Mental Wellbeing and Psychology

Mental Wellbeing and Psychology unpacks the philosophical and psychological need to understand ourselves through an exploration of historical archives and artistic creativity. It focuses on some practical, evidence-based approaches to developing mental wellbeing.

The book uses phenomenological psychology to explore the materials developed by the Stiwdio Arts Group and offers an understanding of their lifeworld experiences, recognising that these are embodied and perceived within a temporal and relational place. It offers examples for developing mental health and wellbeing interventions for charities, private care and the NHS. It provides an evidence base for the use of creativity and historical resources in mental health care.

This book will be of great interest for academics, researchers and post-graduate students in the field of mental wellbeing, nursing and mental health nursing, occupational therapy and social work.

Sue Barker has been a mental health nurse for over 36 years and a chartered psychologist for 25 years. She is currently working as a freelance mental well-being educator.

Louise Jensen is the project lead for the Stiwdio Arts Group, UK.

Hamed Al Battashi is a lecturer in mental health in Oman. He is currently doing his Ph.D with the University of Case Western, USA.

Advances in Mental Health Research series

Books in this series:

Narratives of Art Practice and Mental Wellbeing
Reparation and Connection
Olivia Sagan

Video and Filmmaking as Psychotherapy
Research and Practice
Edited by Joshua L. Cohen and J. Lauren Johnson with Penelope P. Orr

Schizotypy
New Dimensions
Edited by Oliver Mason and Gordon Claridge

The Prevention of Suicide in Prison
Cognitive Behavioural Approaches
Edited by Daniel Pratt

Narratives of Recovery from Mental Illness
The Role of Peer Support
Mike Watts and Agnes Higgins

Supervision and Treatment Experiences of Probationers with Mental Illness
Analyses of Contemporary Issues in Community Corrections
Babatunde Oluwaseun Adekson, Ph.D.

Mental Wellbeing and Psychology
The Role of Art and History in Self Discovery and Creation
Sue Barker with Louise Jensen and Hamed Al Battashi

Mental Wellbeing and Psychology

The Role of Art and History in Self Discovery and Creation

Sue Barker with Louise Jensen and
Hamed Al Battashi

Routledge
Taylor & Francis Group
LONDON AND NEW YORK

First published 2020
by Routledge
2 Park Square, Milton Park, Abingdon, Oxon OX14 4RN

and by Routledge
52 Vanderbilt Avenue, New York, NY 10017

Routledge is an imprint of the Taylor & Francis Group, an informa business

British Library Cataloguing-in-Publication Data
A catalogue record for this book is available from the British Library

Library of Congress Cataloging-in-Publication Data
A catalog record has been requested for this book

ISBN: 978-1-138-34951-3 (hbk)
ISBN: 978-0-429-43431-0 (ebk)

Typeset in Bembo
by Wearset Ltd, Boldon, Tyne and Wear

This book is dedicated to Kevin Jensen, Khalil Al Battashi and all those who facilitate our flourishing.

Breathe deep, fly high, seek peace.

Contents

Figures

Tables

Boxes

Acknowledgements

I would like to thank my husband **Kevin Jensen**, for his continued support for all my endeavours. He has been leaping into the unknown with me over the last few years, encouraging the development of the Stiwdio Arts project and picking me up whenever my confidence has hit the floor. I continue to be grateful for his wise words and wonderful, creative practicality.

I would like to dedicate my writing to my brother, **Khalil Al Battashi**, to thank him for his continuous encouragement and thought provoking discussions. He has always been a role model for me.

I would like to thank my husband, **Julian Barker**, for his faithfulness, sense of duty and encouragement to pick myself up when I fall down so that I can reach for the stars.

For Collingwood project

The Stiwdio Arts Group would like to thank the **Cardiff University Special Collections and Archives** for inviting us to explore the Collingwood Collection, the 'Explore your Archives' initiative for making it possible, and also to the **R.G. Collingwood Society** and to the **Collingwood family members** themselves, who have chosen to share such a wealth of documents and materials for us to learn from and to gain an insight into this amazing family, speaking to us from across the years, particularly through their art.

For Rookwood project

Special thanks to all of those who helped the 'Through the Trees' project flourish including:

Cardiff and Vale Health Charity who have sponsored the project, and to **Simone Joslyn** and the **Creative Arts in Health team** who helped realise the initiative from the beginning.

The **reception staff** at **Rookwood Hospital,** the medical records officer, **Kelvyn Davies,** and **staff** and **patients from wards 4 and 5 and the therapies department**.

The **Hospital Chaplaincy**, and in particular **Reverend Rachel Lewis**, who has given help and support every step of the way and who has kindly allowed us to be in the beautiful Rookwood Chapel.

Anthony Denning from the voluntary organisation, Mensheds, who very kindly built the frames for the exhibition and chairs for the grounds.

Kevin Jensen for his creative carpentry and **Lucy Jensen** for her pyrographic skills in the making of the beautiful signage for the Trail of Trees around the Rookwood grounds.

Chapter 1

Introduction

Why mental wellbeing now?

Mental health and mental wellbeing have become 'hot', even 'sexy', topics in contemporary society despite the discrimination and stigma still associated with long-term mental illnesses. This has been proliferated by the involvement of celebrities and politicians 'coming out' as having mental illnesses or being mentally unwell due to addictions, phobias or someone close to them having dementia. It has been further promoted within the media due to the involvement of the younger members of the UK Royal family through the Heads Together charity. The rates of suicide in the UK have been fairly stable but there has been an increase amongst young men in Scotland despite government initiatives (Samaritans 2018). Globally the highest rates of suicide are in Lithuania (1), Russia (2), Guyana (3), South Korea (4) and Belarus (5), with the US at (27) and UK at (78) (World Population Review 2019).

Alongside governmental and charity concerns, many individuals are also trying to find new ways of developing their wellbeing and resilience in what is considered a rapidly changing and pressurised culture. Wellbeing can even be found to be a pressing issue in the classroom with the *Guardian* newspaper stating, "With mental health problems on the rise in classrooms, we're bringing happiness inspectors into schools and developing a GCSE in wellbeing" (Cope 2017). The current National Institute of Health and Clinical Excellence (NICE) consultations on social, emotional and mental wellbeing in primary and secondary education, school-based interventions, physical and mental health and wellbeing promotion and the Mental Health Foundation Campaign 'Mental health is not extracurricular – make it count' all demonstrate the current concern for mental wellbeing of young people.

The concern is not just for young people's mental health and wellbeing; the highest suicide rates in the UK are in middle age (ONS 2018). There is concern from both statutory and non-statutory agents, with NICE consultations on mental wellbeing at work, and social work interventions for adults with complex needs including learning disabilities and mental health, decision making and mental capacity. Charities such as Mind and Rethink developed the

Time to Change campaign leading to the 'Ask Twice Campaign', and 'In Your Corner'. This is alongside the LADbible (UOKM8?), 'Mental Health Minute' on 300 radio stations, Wired UK and See Me (Scotland). There are also many purely online resources such as #realconvo (in US) and #HereForYou.

Given all this input and resources there is obviously great concern, particularly in Western societies, about mental wellbeing. The evidence base for these is said to be limited by methodological issues and Leckey (2011) states there is a need to define mental wellbeing but it is acknowledged that a number of approaches are helpful. The Stiwdio Arts Group did not set out to change the world; it was just hoped that a few people could be supported with limited resources to improve how they felt about themselves and the world. After the first couple of projects it appeared to all involved this was happening. It was agreed that it felt good and whilst what was happening could not be described as adhering to a traditional research approach for justification, and no one wanted to change that, a different way of explaining and understanding was sought.

What is phenomenological psychology and why use it?

The focus of phenomenology is a 'returning to thing itself' as identified by Edmund Husserl, the founding father. It is "the study of human experience and the way in which things are perceived as they appear to consciousness" (Langdridge 2007: 10). Phenomenology is a family of research methods, but they all are built on the foundations of Husserl's writings and teaching. Whereas the focus of psychology, which also is an umbrella term for several different perspectives, is the science of the human mind, the way people think, feel, behave and interact. Therefore, *the focus of phenomenological psychology is people's perceptions of the world in which they live and what this means to them; their lived (lifeworld) experiences.*

Within phenomenology there are several essential features which occur in most of their methods:

- Intentionality
- Noema and noesis
- Epoche
- Phenomenological reduction
- Imaginative variation
- Essences

Intentionality

The meaning of this term, in phenomenology, is not the same as the regular dictionary definition which states that intentionality is a goal orientated or consciously motivated desire to undertake a certain behaviour. For example, I intended to climb the mountain; my intention is to ride a bike. For Husserl intentionality describes how the mind works; whenever the person is conscious the consciousness is focused towards something (it is aware of something). It is never conscious but unaware (this is to be sub/unconscious). For example, I wake up from sleep with my partner beside me, a clock near my ear and a myriad of other things available to my senses but my intentionality is focused on the bedroom window where I can see the weak morning light seeping through, and I am mostly oblivious to the rest of my surroundings.

Intentionality allows the researcher or philosopher to sidestep whether something is subjective or objective; it is a recognition that there is something that arrives to the conscious or mind that is then processed, perceptually, into the everyday experience of it. It is the relationship between consciousness and the world that is of concern to phenomenologists. The mind and body are not separate; the mind and body are one and things appear to the mind through the body. Perceptions are grounded in people's bodies in relation to the environment in which they live. For psychology this means instead of searching for individual thought patterns and cognitive processes phenomenological psychologists explore experiences, how these are perceived and what meaning is made of them.

Noema and noesis

Noema refers to what is experienced and noesis is the way in which it is experienced. Despite this division the two are intrinsically linked, for example if we return to my waking to focus on the morning light coming through the window. I initially just see the light and perceive it as light in my conscious awareness; light is the noema but the process of noesis offers further possibilities of understanding and perceiving the noema. The noema also provides more information for the development of my understanding of the noesis and further understanding of the noema. Phenomenologists focus on the experience as lived by the person through their perceptions of their world: "we understand the person in the act of perceiving the world" (Langdridge 2007: 17).

Epoche

Epoche, bracketing or bridling, is an attitudinal shift where the researcher or philosopher attempts to abstain from presumptions and preconceived ideas of what might be found. Within traditional research this is achieved through seeking the null hypothesis and replicable studies. The core stance with epoche is one of doubt: doubting what is thought to be known, particularly of what has been called the natural attitude. The natural attitude is the basic way of understanding the world with or without conscious effort but with all pre-learnt suppositions intact.

The use of epoche enables a description of the things themselves by putting on one side the natural attitude. There has been debate over whether epoche can be achieved. Husserl believed that it could be achieved through transcendental philosophical reduction whereas Heidegger and the existentialists believed that whilst it was a good discipline to try to achieve epoche it was not totally achievable. They state that a person is part of the world; they are not separate from it and therefore cannot stand outside it to describe it.

Phenomenological reduction

Another type of attitudinal shift is phenomenological reduction. Whether phenomenologists believe that transcendental reduction can occur or not they all attempt phenomenological reduction which Husserl states can be achieved at different levels and has different types. The deepest level is transcendental but psychologists such as Giorgi and Giorgi (2003) state that phenomenological psychological reduction is sufficient for psychology and health care. This attitude, whilst attempting to bracket the natural attitudes, accepts presences are exactly what they are described as, but no claim is made that they are exactly what they present themselves to be.

Imaginative variation

The first steps to undertaking a study using phenomenological psychology are to assume two attitudes: a psychological perspective and phenomenological psychological reduction. Within these attitudes the stories (data) are read and reread and meaning units are intuited. The intuited meaning units are then transformed into psychologically relevant terms using imaginative variation. Imaginative variation involves exploring all the ways in which a meaning could be expressed whilst retaining its meaning. This sometimes leads to meaning units becoming larger and sometimes they can be reduced to a single word.

Essences

The essence or essences are the core elements of the meaning of a phenomenon. It is the structure underlying the phenomenon. These can be attributed to an individual or termed universal when they are usually labelled eidetic intuition.

Phenomenological psychology therefore offers a way to understand people and their experiences of the world; people's experiences of the world are embodied and perceived within a temporal and relational place. It also offers a method to explicate new understandings and meanings through attitudinal changes (psychological perspective and phenomenological psychological reduction) and within this epoche to intuit meanings within descriptions from the natural attitude.

This does, though, pose a problem for contemporary society where evidence-based practice is formulated into a hierarchy and metanalysis of randomised controlled trial has the 'gold star'. At this point it might be pertinent to consider what evidence or knowledge and how this might be gained.

Ways of knowing?

Generally, when people consider what knowledge is, they identify pieces of information that have been received through reading, watching or listening to others. This is promulgated within contemporary society through the value given to high level empirical evidence in clinical practice and academia, the questions asked in intelligence tests, compulsory education, television quizzes, etc.

As long ago as 1978 Barbara Carper established four ways or patterns of knowing, which she labelled Empirical, Personal, Ethical and Aesthetic.

- Empirical knowing – the understanding of knowledge derived from the traditional scientific approach.
- Personal – the understanding of knowledge developed from self-knowledge or understanding. It is about gaining empathy for another person's experience. It is knowledge that can be gained through imagining self in the other's position to understand their experience.
- Ethical – the understanding of knowledge is gained by exploring and understanding the experience or situation through questioning of choices and their consequences.
- Aesthetic – the understanding of knowledge here is referred to as a consideration of art and beauty but it is about the sensing or perceiving of something and might be labelled intuition.

(Adapted from Barker 2016: 61–62)

Carper's ways of knowing provide a framework to explore a situation or experience in greater depth and to move away from a purely scientific or empirical way of knowing. She facilitated with this work the development of reflective practice and an acknowledgement that caring is an art, not just a science, in the same way that Freud and Rogers have done with psychological understanding. She also opened more widely the exploration of the use of the aesthetic or intuition in care.

Patricia Benner (1984) in her book *From Novice to Expert* described expert nurses as using their intuition in clinical practice. She explained that as practitioners develop experience, their conscious knowledge of practice becomes tacit (intuitive). They move from novice (unconscious incompetence), to advanced beginner (conscious incompetence), to competent (consciously competent), to proficient (competent), to unconscious competence (expert). She later went on to label this as development 'patterning' (Benner 2010).

Carper's aesthetic way of knowing has been further developed by a number of writers using a number of terms: 'intuition' (Morse *et al.* 1994; Davis-Floyd and Davis 1996), 'tacit knowing and knowledge' (Benner and Wrubel 1989), 'embodied knowledge' (Polkinghorne 2004), 'reflexivity and reflection in action' (Johns 1998, 2004, 2013) and 'emotional intelligence' (Goleman 1995).

Benner and Wrubel (1989) described intuition as how we 'know how', which they identify as tacit knowledge or knowledge that lacks an explanation but is relational; it is embedded in the situation. Hildingsson and Häggström (1999) referred to intuition as an interpretive tool as used by midwives to identify the needs of women, in a similar way to the nurses in Morse *et al.*'s study (1994). Johns (2004) advocated reflection as a process for uncovering this tacit knowing or knowledge which he recognised as intuition.

Three ways of intuitive knowing have been identified:

- Intuition based on practice experience – this can be seen to refer to where practitioners develop an inner knowing through experience and may be what Benner is suggesting in her expert nurses.
- Intuition based on spiritual awareness – this appears to be where the practitioner received a word or message, which could be a vision that is accounted for as a spiritual experience.
- Intuition based on connectiveness – practitioners are using their intimate knowledge of the person to understand them, their needs and their possible outcomes.

These different types of intuition, though, are seen to be overlapping and interrelated (Ólafsdóttir 2009). Intuition based on connectiveness is 'an awareness creating relationship' or 'tuning in' (Ólafsdóttir 2009) providing a 'relational way of understanding or knowing' (Todres 2008). This is a way of knowing that is related to the lifeworld and is concerned with relationships and connection. It establishes a close relationship as part of a living situation (Todres 2008).

Summary and conclusion

The materials developed by the Stiwdio Arts Group have been explored using phenomenological psychology. This chapter therefore offers an understanding of the participants' experiences of their world, recognising that these are embodied and perceived within a temporal and relational place. This was undertaken by developing meaning whilst undergoing the attitudinal changes related to the psychological perspective and phenomenological psychological reduction. Within this epoche meanings were gathered through imaginative variation and intuitive reading of the reflections, evaluations and poems from the natural attitude. The intuition or aesthetic way of knowing accessed here was believed to have elements from all the types of intuition identified above. The intuition was based on connectiveness, a 'tuning in' to the personal narratives which provided a 'relational way of understanding or knowing'. Spiritual and experiential or personal knowing can also be seen to be part of the development of meaning, as despite residing within the epoche as much as I could, I am a spiritual person and my experience of being a person within the world cannot totally be denied when reading others' natural attitude narratives. This can be seen in that I could not have undertaken the reading without accessing part of my experience, in this case my ability to read and understand the English language in a certain way.

I cannot therefore claim what is presented here by me as my perceptual understanding is an accurate portrait of the participants' lifeworld experiences, but they and I felt that it was a close fit.

Phenomenological theorists such as Todres, Galvin, Gendlin and Giorgi have all provided a language with which to express the meanings derived from this understanding of the participants' experiences. Terms like felt sense, soulful space, insiderness, temporality and dwelling mobility have all been useful in my attempt to express my understanding.

Overview of the chapters

Chapter 1 – Introduction

This chapter offers a rationale and justification for the approach taken within this book and why mental wellbeing is a suitable topic for this type of discussion now. A brief description is provided on what phenomenological psychology is, leading to a short explanation of the different ways of knowing. One of these, aesthetic (intuitive) ways of knowing, was highlighted as a component of the phenomenological psychology approach.

The second half of the chapter provides a brief summary of the rest of the chapters in the book, finishing with the boundaries and limitations.

Chapter 2 – Mental wellbeing

This chapter starts with an exploration of the definitions of mental wellbeing and whilst it is considered intangible many attempts have been made to define, describe and measure it.

The main theorists within psychology are briefly described along with what they bring to the discussion on wellbeing. The chapter then moves on to consider more specific wellbeing theories developed by psychologists including Deiner's tripartite model of subjective wellbeing, Carol Ryff's six-factor model of psychological wellbeing and Corey Keyes' flourishing. This leads on to what might be considered a more philosophical understanding.

A brief description ensues of the philosophical understanding of wellbeing from Socrates and Plato, who understand wellbeing as a type of mystic rapture, into a discussion of whether wellbeing is based on happiness or doing the right thing. Following this is the need to consider place, context and society using anthropological and cultural literature. Within this cultural exploration the impact of religion, faith and beliefs is considered, and four boxes provided offering a description of wellbeing from the four major religious groups, along with some first-person explanations of what wellbeing is to their specific religious group.

Philosophically, anthropologically and psychologically the key to understanding wellbeing is through the experience of joy mediated by the body, truth, beauty and/or the divine; this makes suffering in life experiences meaningful and worthwhile.

Chapter 3 – Embodied subjective self and resilience

Self is explored in this chapter through the dichotomy of objective or social theories and subjective self. These are linked with a brief consideration of selfhood and the chapter finishes with an overview of two ways in which self-knowledge and associated mental wellbeing could be increased: resilience and self-compassion.

There are many social theories of the self, also known as self-concept or personality. Here just a few of the most popular ones have been explored. All these social psychological understandings of the self have their foundations in the behavioural perspective. A developmental approach has been taken to describe them with the earlier theories of behaviourism first leading into social learning theories and symbolic interaction. All these social theories support a cognitive psychological definition of the self or personality as the relatively stable traits or characteristics demonstrated by a person over time.

This definition of the self or personality is considered insufficient for the writers of this chapter who find it to be lacking in its sense of humanity. The second half of the chapter explores subjective self and the other (excluding cognitive behavioural ones) main psychological perspectives, psychodynamic and humanistic. It also outlines their philosophical underpinning. This leads to a more phenomenological psychological perspective definition of self or personality; *it is the interaction between an individual's 'felt sense' which provides meaning through embodied relational knowing and the world in which the person lives in time and space.*

Chapter 4 – History, temporality and culture

A sense of wellbeing is fundamentally linked to the person's sense of identity within time and place, historically and culturally. It is an act of self-identification which needs to be an authentic interpretation of the relationship between the existence of the individual and a world that makes sense. This relationship may exist in a myriad of ways due to the number of different social orders and practices in historically, spatially and socially determined circumstances (Friedman 1992). Fuchs (2013) also recognises the importance of these from a phenomenological philosophical perspective. He identifies three features of temporality: implicit subjective temporality (the individual unconsciously aware of time), explicit subjective temporality (the individual consciously aware of time) and intersubjective temporality (a shared sense of time).

Malpas and Tilley, phenomenological archaeologists, use their senses to engage with places as they move around landscapes which assist with investigation into social and cultural meaning that might be associated with it. Tilley highlights that whilst traditional archaeologists focus on and describe the physical world it is still experienced by the person on a sensory and emotional level. The place and its history are intertwined with humans; it is a two-way relationship – people influence the place and the place influences the person within time.

Culture impacts on the way the person perceives the world, their worldview; it is the outward expression of shared meaning which occurs at a particular time and place. Cultures can be now be mega experienced at global level or macro at a country or societal level, or even micro (subculture) level such as a racial or religious group. They all have underpinning ideologies which can also affect the person's sense of themselves and their ability to experience wellbeing.

The rich tapestry of life can only be appreciated by embodied interaction with the world and each other including a recognition that experiences occur in time and space. The culture, which is time, place and ideology bound, can when lived in dramatically influence how and if a person experiences a sense of wellbeing.

Chapter 5 – Creativity and wellbeing

Creativity as a concept was initially identified as a 'fuzzy soft concept' but at the same time dynamic and exciting. Despite this incongruity there have been a number of descriptions of creativity. Psychologists tend to agree, though, that creativity is to do with the ability to use imagination and make things, and it is also recognised as a human need and part of normal personality development. Creativity is not only desirable for wellbeing, it is necessary for mental health to avoid burnout.

The World Health Organisation acknowledges a set of social determinants of health and wellbeing which can be worked with using creativity to increase wellbeing. The social determinants are the circumstances in which people are born, grow, live, work and age. They are influenced by the distribution of money, power and resources at global, national and local levels. The evidence indicates that creative activities can have a healing and protective effect on mental wellbeing but there are limitations to the current evidence base.

Human flourishing is another term for the concept of wellbeing and has been used by a number of theorists, particularly the positive psychologists. The research undertaken in this area offers another perspective on the aims for creativity and wellbeing. Tay *et al.*'s (2018) framework for flourishing provides four areas of influence:

1. Neurological/physiological/psychological reactions
2. Psychological competencies
3. General wellbeing effects
4. Positive normative outcomes

Alternatively, NEF (Foresight 2008) provides five mechanisms for change: Connect, Be active, Take notice, Keep learning, Give. Another model for creativity and wellbeing was developed by Natalie Rogers, daughter of Carl Rogers, who offers the conditions for creativity based on his foundational theory. Rogers (1993: 14) states:

> The Conditions that foster creativity
>
> 1. Psychological safety
>   a. Accepting the individual as of unconditional worth
>   b. Providing a climate in which external evaluation is absent
>   c. Understanding empathetically
> 2. Psychological freedom
> 3. Offering stimulating and challenging experiences

Whilst these models can guide services, health care has provided art therapy for many years and more recently this type of social prescribing has been incorporated into statutory services.

Chapter 6 – Stiwdio Arts Group

The Stiwdio Arts Group was developed with some understanding of the evidence base but also using a tentative phenomenological approach. Each project started with a pilot to check structure, media and resources. They were then created within a local context. Whilst there are some essential key features in structure, process and outcomes, each project has its unique constituents in place and time. The phenomenon cannot be precisely reproduced due to these unique features but the lived experiences within the participants, leaders and members of the public can be learnt from in the promotion of wellbeing.

All the projects received evaluations that included the following:

- More satisfied with life, more happiness
- Creations
- Opportunity to learn
- Company of others
- Time to focus

In addition, the individual variations included:

'Artist in the Making' Collingwood project

- Time to engage with warmth and comfort
- Freedom

'Through the Trees' Rookwood project

- Love, care and hope
- Time for silence and laughter
- Engaging, intriguing, magical and relaxing

Chapter 7 – Evaluations, reflections and creations

The working definition from previous philosophy, anthropology and psychology literature led to an acceptance that the *key to understanding wellbeing is through the experience of joy mediated by the body, truth, beauty and/or the divine, which makes suffering in life experiences meaningful and worthwhile.* As this is a subjective experience, self also required a working definition which was established to be: *the interaction between an individual's 'felt sense' which provides meaning through embodied relational knowing and the world in which the person lives in time and space.*

These definitions provided a foundation for understanding the evaluations, reflections, pictures and creative writing from two of the Stiwdio Arts Group projects. These two were used due to the amount of material available to provide some understanding of the participants' experiences.

Both projects were led by Louise and structured in a similar way and therefore the main differences in the projects were focus, time and place. The reflections have been left as the individuals' written stories so that the reader can draw out their own interpretations and meanings; they leave the reader to develop, in turn, their own story.

Despite a lack of interpretation offered here it is clear that the phenomenon of mental wellbeing is an embodied experience within a certain sense of time and place that can be enlivened by creativity.

Chapter 8 – Phenomenological psychological lifeworld experiences

Mental wellbeing is subjective which makes it difficult to precisely define and measure. Many attempts have been made to do so but each falls short of providing a neat impression of the rich tapestry that facilitates this individual experience. Four categories of keys to mental wellbeing and ten dimensions are identified here but all are acknowledged as inadequate. Despite their inadequacy they were useful in identifying that the evaluations and reflections generated from the Stiwdio Arts projects did demonstrate achievement of mental wellbeing for the participants in the contemporary understanding of what this means.

It is acknowledged there is more to experiences than can be objectively stated and measured; this was also true for the relationship between self and mental wellbeing with personality being defined here as *the interaction between an individual's 'felt sense' which provides meaning through embodied relational knowing and the world in which the person lives in time and space.*

Through felt sense, self-recognition and acceptance of one's self including personal vulnerability may be the first step towards self-compassion and mental wellbeing. Mental wellbeing occurs through the ability to enter a moment in time and space, a *'soulful space'* where the person can accept themselves, in their entirety, including their vulnerability, to gain a deep sense of who they are and who they are becoming. It is through acceptance of self and others within a state of temporal and spatial *dwelling mobility*, that people need to understand themselves and their personal present, history and future possibilities but also how this interweaves with their sense of others and others' history.

Therapeutic approaches such as resilience training, compassion-focused therapy, art therapy and focusing can all add to understanding and the development of mental wellbeing, but 'presence' would appear to be key. Presence means to be truly accepting and accepted, to be loved and to love and in the moment experiencing a sense of joy and peace, acknowledging things will change, knowing it was achieved in the past, in the now and the future is full of possibilities.

Through the Stiwdio Arts Group projects and associated conceptual analysis, mental wellbeing is conceived as *lived through experiences of shared joy mediated by the body, truth, beauty and/or the divine; this makes suffering in life experiences meaningful and life worthwhile.*

The Stiwdio Arts Group's achievements can be understood as an integration of different psychological perspectives under an umbrella of psychological phenomenology, accepting the current philosophical thinking relating to self-acknowledgement and self-acceptance and recognising that personal experiences are contextual. This has been achieved through creative and historical engagement and facilitation of dwelling mobility. The leaders developed this therapeutic environment where human flourishing was propagated.

Boundaries and limitations

In this book only the words have been explored using the lens of the psychological perspective and phenomenological techniques. The phenomenological language has been used to explicate the meanings as they provided the best fit for the writers. It may be that others would have used a different style of language or perhaps a sociological lens. There has been no attempt to translate or interpret the artwork in the written language as this is not within the skill set of the authors.

Spiritual and experiential or personal knowing can also be seen to be part of the development of meaning as despite residing within the epoche as much as the authors could, they are spiritual people and their experiences of being a person within the world cannot totally be denied when reading others' natural attitude narratives. This can be seen in that we could not have undertaken the reading without accessing part of their experiences, in this case, their ability to read and understand the English language in a certain way.

We cannot therefore claim what is presented here by us as our perceptual understanding is an accurate portrait of the participants' lifeworld experiences, but they and we felt that it was a close fit.

Phenomenological theorists such as Todres, Galvin, Gendlin and Giorgi have all provided a language with which to express the meanings derived from this understanding of the participants' experiences. Terms like felt sense, soulful space, insiderness, temporality and dwelling mobility have all been useful in our attempt to express our understanding.

Summary

Chapter 1 has provided an introduction to this book. It initially gave a rationale and justification for the approach taken including why mental wellbeing is a suitable topic for discussion now. This was followed by a brief description of phenomenology psychology leading to a short explanation of the different ways of knowing developed by Carper (1978). One of these, aesthetic (intuitive) ways of knowing, was highlighted as a component of the phenomenological psychology method of research.

The summary and conclusion of the first half of this chapter was provided which explained the foundational concepts of phenomenological psychology and ways of knowing that have been used within the book. The second half of the chapter offered a brief summary of the rest of the chapters in the book, finishing with the boundaries and limitations.

References

Barker, S. 2016. *Psychology for Nurses and Health Care Practitioners to Support Compassionate Care*. London: Sage.

Benner, P. 1984. *From Novice to Expert*. Menlo Park, California: Addison-Wesley.

Benner, P., Sutphen, M., Leonard, V., Day, R. 2010. *Educating Nurses: A Call to Radical Transformation*. San Francisco: Wiley Imprint.

Benner, P., Wrubel, J. 1989. *The Primacy of Caring: Stress and coping in Health and Illness*. Menlo Park, California: Addison-Wesley.

Carper, B.A. 1978. "Fundamental Patterns of Knowing in Nursing", *Advances in Nursing Science*, 1, 1, 13–24.

Cope, A. 2017. "With Mental Health Problems on the Rise in Classrooms, We're Bringing Happiness Inspectors into Schools and Developing a GCSE in Wellbeing", *Guardian*, August 25, www.theguardian.com/teacher-network/2017/aug/25/childrens-mental-health-its-time-to-put-wellbeing-on-the-curriculum.

Davis-Floyd, R., Davis, E. 1996. "Intuition as Authoritative Knowledge in Midwifery and Home Births", *Medical Anthropology Quarterly*, 10, 2, 237–269.

Foresight. 2008. Foresight Mental Capital and Wellbeing Project: Final Project Report. London: The Government Office for Science. Retrieved from: www.bis.gov.uk/foresight/our-work/projects/current-projects/mental-capitaland-wellbeing.

Friedman, J. 1992. "The Past in the Future: History and the Politics of Identity", *American Anthropologist,* 94, 4, new series, 837–859. Retrieved from: www.jstor.org/stable/680224.

Fuchs, T. 2013. "Temporality and psychopathology", *Phenomenology and the Cognitive Sciences*, 12, 75–104. DOI: 10.1007/s11097-010-9189-4.

Giorgi, A., Giorgi, B. 2003. "Phenomenology". *In*: Smith, J.A. (Ed.) *Qualitative Psychology, a Practical Guide to Research Methods*. London: Sage.

Goleman, D. 1995. *Emotional Intelligence*. New York: Basic Books.

Hildingsson, I., Häggström, T. 1999. "Midwives' Lived Experiences of Being Supportive to Prospective Mothers/Parents During Pregnancy", *Midwifery*, 15, 82–91.

Johns, C. 1998. "Caring Through a Reflective Lens: Giving Meaning to Being a Reflective Practitioner", *Nursing Inquiry*, 5, 18–24.

Johns, C. (Ed.) 2004. *Becoming a Reflective Practitioner. A Reflective and Holistic Approach to Clinical Nursing, Practice Development and Clinical Supervision* (second edition). Oxford: Blackwell Publishing.

Johns, C. (Ed.) 2013. *Becoming a Reflective Practitioner,* fourth edition. New Jersey/Chichester: Wiley-Blackwell.

Langdridge, D. 2007. *Phenomenological Psychology, Theory, Research and Method*. Essex: Pearson, Prentice Hall, pp. 10, 17.

Leckey, J. 2011. "The Therapeutic Effectiveness of Creative Activities on Mental Well-being: A Systematic Review of the Literature", *Journal of Psychiatric and Mental Health Nursing,* 18, 6, 501–509.

Morse, J.M., Bottorff, J.L., Hutchinson, S. 1994. "The Phenomenology of Comfort", *Journal of Advanced Nursing*, 20, 189–195.

Office for National Statistics. 2018. Suicides in the UK: 2017 Registrations. www.ons.gov.uk/peoplepopulationandcommunity/birthsdeathsandmarriages/deaths/bulletins/suicidesintheunitedkingdom/2017registrations.

Ólafsdóttir, Ó.Á. 2009. "Inner Knowing and Emotions in the Midwife-Woman Relationship". *In*: Hunter, B. and Deery, R. (Eds.) *Emotions in Midwifery and Reproduction*. Hampshire: Palgrave Macmillan, pp. 192–210.

Polkinghorne, D. 2004. *Practice and the Human Sciences: The Case for a Judgement-based Practice of Care*. New York: State University of New York, pp. 129–150.

Rogers, N. 1993. *The Creative Connection. Expressive Arts in Healing*. California: Science and Behaviour Books Inc., p. 14.

Samaritans, 2018. Samaritans Suicide Statistics Report 2018. www.samaritans.org/about-samaritans/research-policy/suicide-facts-and-figures/.

Tay, L., Pawelski, J.O., Keith, M.G. 2018. "The Role of the Arts and Humanities in Human Flourishing: A Conceptual Model", *The Journal of Positive Psychology*, 13, 3, 215–225. DOI: 10.1080/17439760.2017.1279207.

Todres, L. 2008. "Being with That: The Relevance of Embodied Understanding for Practice", *Qualitative Health Research*, 18, 11, 1566–1573.

World Population Review. 2019. Suicide Rate by Country 2019. http://worldpopulationreview.com/countries/suicide-rate-by-country/.

Chapter 2

Mental wellbeing

Introduction

Wellbeing is a growing area of research and despite being a 'hot' topic in contemporary society it lacks clear definition (Dodge *et al.* 2012). Many people are trying to find new ways of developing their wellbeing and resilience in what is considered a rapidly changing and pressurised culture. Alongside funded research and counselling focused on wellbeing can be found hordes of self-help books and websites all of which purport to increase resilience and wellbeing. Some of the more popular current trends in achieving this are through exercising mindfulness, meditating and physical activity which are clearly outlined in the popular press. From colouring books to meditation and exercise, mental wellbeing practice is emphatically promoted.

The *Sun* newspaper headlined "Increasing awareness – What is mindfulness? Mindfulness is knowing what is happening inside and outside ourselves moment by moment" (Lake 2018). Wellbeing can even be found to be a pressing issue in the classroom with the *Guardian* newspaper stating, "With mental health problems on the rise in classrooms, we're bringing happiness inspectors into schools and developing a GCSE in wellbeing" (Cope 2017). Influenced by media hype and the increasing number of helpful tools in developing wellbeing, in contemporary society it remains unlikely that any will provide the panacea for all modern 'ills'.

Current culture within Western societies has moved towards a focus on wellbeing, with less promotion of holistic health which can be seen as a move away from health per se to wellbeing. This may be, at least, in part due to economic and political processes as whilst life expectancy has increased morbidity rates have continued leading to more people living with health problems (Gov. UK 2017a). Although this trend does see fluctuations, for example in 2015 23 of the 28 countries in the EU's life expectancy at birth reduced slightly, the trend continues (Gov. UK 2017b). Both social and health care in the UK offer definitions of and promote wellbeing orientated practice. The Social Care Institute of Excellence (SCIE 2005) identified that wellbeing refers to a subjective assessment of feelings about life experiences. The Department of Health (2007: 99) offered the following definition:

> Well-being is the subjective state of being healthy, happy, contented, comfortable and satisfied with one's quality of life. It includes physical, material, social, emotional ("happiness"), and development and activity dimensions.

The problem this definition poses is 'What is quality of life?' for clinicians and researchers alike but it is accepted as central to many explorations of wellbeing. Notwithstanding these attempts at definition, wellbeing does not appear to correlate with physical health as the oldest and youngest within society have the highest rates of wellbeing but older people also have the highest rates of ill health (Barker 2013). Further, Thomas (2009) stated wellbeing is intangible and difficult to define; he also argued it is even harder to measure. This is a common situation with psychological concepts or constructs related to subjectivity.

Another issue with the term 'quality of life' is that in literature it can be found to be used interchangeably with 'wellbeing'; this has made defining wellbeing conceptually muddy (Morrow and Mayall 2009: 221). Despite this ill-defined use of the term, the concept of wellbeing has enabled psychologists and other allied health and care professionals to 'de-medicalise' the concept of health, as can be seen in mental health care which has more recently, in Western cultures, focused on a 'recovery approach' to interventions.

Whilst a generally accepted scientific definition is elusive, there are acceptable descriptions of wellbeing. It is described as two dimensional; it can be viewed as both a subjective experience and objectively observed. These pose different challenges for researchers with each falling within a different philosophical approach to understanding: epistemology (the nature of knowledge) and ontology (the nature of being).

Subjective wellbeing (or personal wellbeing) is how people think and feel about their own wellbeing and includes aspects such as life satisfaction (evaluation), positive emotions (hedonic), and whether their life is meaningful (eudaemonic). Subjective wellbeing is an exploration of the person's experiences, their sense of being. Whilst it can be measured using a positivist approach through self-report and certain observational methodologies these can still be criticised by ontologists as missing the essential richness of human experience.

Whereas objective wellbeing is generally based on assumptions about basic human needs (for example Maslow's hierarchy of needs) and rights (such as the Human Rights Act), it includes elements such as adequate food, physical health, education, safety etc. Objective wellbeing can also be measured through broader measures (e.g. mortality rates and life expectancy) (Gov. UK 2014). These approaches to wellbeing are problematic as they are preoccupied with identifying the variables that affect (enhance or diminish) wellbeing through the use of pre-existing measurements (Ferraro and Sarmiento Barletti 2016). Imposing this type of intellectual order upon wellbeing, usually biased by affluent Westerners, leads to any unearthing of the layers of meaning of these experiences being removed (Herbert 2000).

Health and social care practitioners and researchers are neither the first nor only interested parties in the exploration of wellbeing despite being predominant in contemporary society. Historically, philosophers, psychologists, anthropologists and sociologists all have had a stake in defining, describing and theorising about wellbeing.

Psychological theories of wellbeing

Psychology, the youngest traditional science, has a history starting in the 1870s but the exploration of the human mind was explored prior to this period, subsumed within philosophy. It developed in the US and Germany. Some of the founding fathers of this new science were Wundt (experimental psychology), Ebbinghaus (memory research), James (pragmatism) and Pavlov (classical conditioning) (Barker 2016).

The writings of one of these early psychologists, William James, included healthy-mindedness (1988 [1902]); as part of this he offered a psychological analysis of religious experiences and stated that the leaders of world religions (Christianity, Islam, Buddhism, Hinduism) were 'morbid-minded'. He wrote this was due to their acceptance that evil always has been and will be in the world. Those James identified as 'healthy-minded' were people who believe evil is not essential. Healthy-mindedness comes from ignoring or reinterpreting evil: turning evil into good. Whether people need religion or can reinterpret themselves is dependent on their temperament. He goes further to suggest that turning evil into good is a mind cure and could be considered a religion (Pawelski 2003).

James continued to write on this topic for almost 60 years and is recognised as a predecessor to the theorising of Carl Rogers. Rogers clearly outlines in his *On Becoming a Person* how wellbeing is linked to leading the good life (Rogers 1961: 186). His humanistic perspective indicates that to become a fully functioning person one needs to be open and trust their personal organistic experiences which will lead to an increasingly existential life.

Since the early writing of James' psychology, psychological publications, research and theories have proliferated leading to differing perspectives and disciplines within the field, with medics and philosophers like Sigmund Freud becoming the founder of a cluster or perspective in psychology. Freud is the founding father of psychodynamic psychology, publishing his book *The Interpretation of Dreams* in 1900, followed by others who were to redevelop his theories such as Jung and Freud's daughter Anna Freud (1927). This perspective was to continue to develop and influence the anthropological work of

Erik Erikson (1950) and the attachment theories of Mary Main (1968), Harry Harlow and John Bowlby (1969).

Behaviourism began shortly after the publication of Freud's book with the experiments of Ivan Pavlov published in 1906 but Pavlov would have described himself as a biologist or natural scientist, not a psychologist. His experiments, though, established an early form of learning theory labelled classical conditioning (learning by association or conditioning reflexes).

It was John E. Watson in 1913 who was to create the perspective of behaviourism which was to include Thorndike's operant conditioning (1911) and Bandura's social learning theory (1963). John B. Watson was to clearly demonstrate the impact of conditioning on a boy called Albert in contrast to other behaviourists who mostly used animals as subjects in their experiments.

Whilst behaviourism is acknowledged as a reaction to psychodynamic theory, cognitive and gestalt psychology are a response to behaviourism. In 1929 Kohler initiated the development of gestalt psychology and in 1932 Jean Piaget the foundations of cognitive psychology. It was not until 1967 that Ulric Neisser founded the perspective of cognitive psychology, but many theories and therapies were to grow out of this, for example:

1957: Festinger – cognitive dissonance
1962: Albert Ellis – rational emotive therapy
1963: Stanley Milgrom – obedience
1966: Julian Rotter – locus of control
1967: Arron Beck – depression
1971: Zimbardo – perceptions of power

As medicine was developing and becoming more technological, a new field of medicine was created called psychiatry, where people could be treated for abnormal psychological functioning. This supported the genesis of biopsychology and neuropsychology where an anatomical or physiological understanding of psychological functioning is explored. Some of the early researchers in this area are Walter B. Cannon (1932) with homeostasis and flight or fight, Noam Chomsky's (1957) Language Acquisition Device.

The humanistic perspective in psychology, whilst having foundations in the earliest writings in psychology, synthesised psychodynamic, behavioural, cognitive and biological theories and added a spiritual element to create a collection of theories called humanistic psychology. The founding fathers of this perspective were Carl Roger (1942) and Abraham Maslow (1954). This perspective was later to be joined by positive psychology, founded by Martin Seligman (1998).

Each of these perspectives offers a different understanding of wellbeing. For psychodynamic theories it is the balancing of the opposing parts of the mind which is achieved through close relationships with others. This can partly be seen to be true for the humanists for whom relationships are key; they state that for a person to become who they are meant to be they need to receive unconditional positive regard which is usually gained from their parents. Relationships are also key for behaviourists, but the process is quite different for them: people need role models so that they can learn how to be most effective to achieve wellbeing. Cognitive, biological and positive psychologists influenced by traditional scientific approaches that provide the foundations for psychology have sought to develop psychological models to understand and measure wellbeing.

Diener: tripartite model of subjective wellbeing

Diener and Suh (1997) indicate that subjective wellbeing consists of three interrelated components: life satisfaction, pleasant affect and unpleasant affect. They offer an understanding that wellbeing involves two psychological processes: affective (mood/emotion) and cognitive (satisfaction evaluation).

Carol Ryff – six-factor model of psychological wellbeing

Likewise, Ryff's early work (Ryff 1989) also identified aspects that constitute wellbeing: autonomy; environmental mastery; positive relationships with others; purpose in life; realisation of potential and self-acceptance. These were later adapted to self-acceptance; purpose in life; environmental mastery; positive relationships; personal growth and autonomy (Ryff and Singer 2008). This work can be seen to be influenced by William James (1902). Given the accepted subjective nature of wellbeing it is likely that individual people will accept some of these constructs and not others.

Corey Keyes: flourishing

Keyes (2002), contemporary of Ryff, stated mental wellbeing has three components: emotional or subjective wellbeing, psychological wellbeing and social wellbeing. Emotional wellbeing concerns subjective aspects of wellbeing, whereas psychological and social wellbeing concerns skills, abilities, and psychological and social functioning. Keyes' model of mental wellbeing has received extensive empirical support across cultures.

Keyes reviewed the dimensions and scales of subjective wellbeing, creating a model of mental wellbeing which he labelled flourishing. Flourishing he identified as functioning optimally or achieving one's potential. Keyes (2002) went on to create criteria to assess whether an individual's life was flourishing using previously validated measures of each of the concepts including the Diagnostic Statistical Manual developed by the American Psychiatric Association to diagnose mental illness.

1 No episodes of major depression in the past year
2 High level of wellbeing as indicated by the meeting all three of the following:
    - High emotional wellbeing, defined by: high positive affect, low negative affect and high life satisfaction
    - High psychological wellbeing defined by achieving at least four out of six of the following: self-acceptance, personal growth, purpose in life, environmental mastery, autonomy, positive relationships
    - High social wellbeing, defined by achieving at least three out of five of the following: social acceptance, actualisation, contribution, coherence, integration.

Seligman: positive psychology

Keyes is categorised as a positive psychologist and Martin Seligman, who is identified as the founder/leader of positive psychology, similarly has written about flourishing in his book entitled *Flourish* (Seligman 2011). In this book he outlines his new 'dynamic' concept of wellbeing in which he identifies that the five elements of his wellbeing theory are: positive emotions, engagement, relationships, meaning and purpose, accomplishment (acronym: PERMA). He states that previously the notion of happiness was the focus of positive psychology to achieve wellbeing but this obscures the true, complex nature of human flourishing. Seligman now thinks the best way to measure wellbeing is flourishing, therefore the goal of positive psychology is to increase flourishing (Seligman 2011).

Whilst Seligman, Corey and Ryff are all psychologists that have followed a path to conceptualise wellbeing as equivalent to human flourishing, there have also been other pathways to a similar understanding.

Philosophical thought related to wellbeing

The ancient Greek philosopher, Aristotle (384–322 BCE), developed the idea of eudaemonia, which is now more commonly translated as 'wellbeing', but it is thought to be more accurately translated as 'human flourishing' or 'prosperity'. He believed this to be the overarching goal of all human actions. Subsequent philosophical approaches built on this, facilitating the exploration of wellbeing through the dialectic of hedonism or utilitarian versus moral or value base focused. Therefore, increased wellbeing was thought to occur either with the greater experience of happiness (hedonism/utilitarianism) or the person's ability to 'do the right thing' (categorical prerogative) but the human goal was always to increase wellbeing.

The word 'hedonism' comes from the Greek word 'delight' but the philosophy is said to reach back as far as Old Babylonian times (2000 to 1600 BCE) and examples can be gained from ancient Egypt during a similar period.

Democritus (460–370 BCE), a pre-Socratic philosopher, stated that the supreme goal of life is 'contentment' or 'cheerfulness' making him probably the first identified philosopher to promote hedonism. A hedonistic school of philosophy was established in the fourth century called the Cyrenaic which became one of the earliest Socratic schools. School, in this sense, was a group of like-minded people, not a building in which learning took place. Hellenistic intellectual processing had a significant impact on the Northern hemisphere, leading to most schools of philosophy being said to have their foundations in Socrates or labelled as pre-Socratic.

The simplest form of hedonism is probably Bentham's; the more pleasantness one can experience, the better life will be, and the more painful the worse it will be. Jeremy Bentham, a well-known hedonist, begins his *Introduction to the Principles of Morals and Legislation* with this statement: "Nature has placed mankind under the governance of two masters, *pain* and *pleasure*. It is for them alone to point out what we ought to do" (2018 [1789]: 11). A hedonist will identify wellbeing as 'the greatest balance of pleasure over pain'. Utilitarianism could also be considered to be in the same category as hedonism but where hedonism is individually focused utilitarianism is more political and community focused.

As with hedonism, wellbeing is also central to moral or ethical and political philosophy but the aim of these schools of thought is to 'live the good life' instead of seeking the most pleasure. The term coined for this by Immanuel Kant (1724–1804), a deontologist, was the 'categorical imperative', which stated that people are naturally moral; they are made by God as moral beings. Therefore, doing the right thing leads to feelings of wellbeing. A strategy that could be adopted in defence of morality as a path to wellbeing is to claim that a person's wellbeing is in some sense constituted by their virtue. This was the approach used in subtly different ways by the three greatest ancient Hellenistic philosophers, Socrates, Plato and Aristotle.

- Socrates: the need for control over basic desires to achieve virtue or wellbeing
- Plato: the need for self-sacrifice to achieve virtue or wellbeing
- Aristotle: the need for promotion of self-care to achieve virtue or wellbeing

Socrates and Plato posited that a sort of 'mystic rapture' provided a sense of wellbeing and that this was primarily to be achieved through philosophy, the understanding of oneself and wisdom. Other moral philosophers identify either a religious or aesthetic interpretation to wellbeing. Christian thinkers state the greatest happiness is the pure vision of God (Thomas Aquinas 1225–1274) and others proclaim that it can be found in a vision of beauty, in music or art (Arthur Schopenhauer 1788–1850). Within this book we will explore all these areas of experiencing mental wellbeing.

Philosophy offers many ideas on what wellbeing is and how it can be achieved but all link to some form of pleasure or contentment. Hedonists and utilitarian philosophers offer an earthy or bodily experience to wellbeing and moral philosophers in a more existential path. Regardless of which philosophical idea is held the key understanding is experience of pleasure through the body, truth, beauty or the divine, which will make the sufferings and tribulations of life experiences meaningful and worthwhile and lead to a sense of wellbeing.

Anthropological/social understandings of wellbeing

Anthropology is the study of people, how they behave and groups in which they live historically through to contemporary societies. Anthropology as with philosophy and psychology can be divided into different theoretical groups or schools. Where social anthropology and cultural anthropology involve the study of norms and values of societies, linguistic anthropological studies focus on how language affects social life. Biological or physical anthropologists examine the biological development of humans in a similar way to evolutionary, developmental and biological psychologists.

Anthropology has been slow in the exploration of wellbeing; mostly this would appear to be due to the perceived subjective nature of the experience (Ferraro *et al.* 2016). Anthropologists usually study groups, cultures and societies by immersing themselves in the culture and engaging with the social behaviours. Even biological and physical anthropologists are unlikely to explore the embodied individual experience. There has, though, along with the early philosophers, been an interest in happiness within anthropology. Many view subjective happiness and wellbeing to have a high correlation, which is similar to the hedonistic philosophers.

Contemporary cultures tend to be divided into two categories in anthropological studies: Western or individualistic cultures and Eastern or collective cultures. All cultures are more complex than this for social and cultural anthropologists, but this binary offers a stereotype that facilitates exploration of these complex systems.

In Western or individualistic cultures happiness tends to be experienced through features that support personal independence, a sense of personal agency and self-expression. In Eastern or collective cultures happiness may be found in an interdependency where individual self is inseparable from significant others. Therefore Eastern cultures are more likely to judge their experiences on the appraisal of others rather than an evaluation of their personal level of pleasant emotions. For example, Japanese societies tend to associate the experience of happiness with interpersonal engagement emotions, such as feeling friendly, whereas those influenced by the hegemony of the United States (US) are more likely to feel happiness through intrapersonal or disengaging emotions such as pride. Whilst the US is considered to fall within a Western culture it has several other significant cultural groups residing within it.

Within the US, Asian Americans demonstrate seeking happiness or wellbeing through doing things to please or approved of by others whereas European Americans are more individualistic in this undertaking. The dichotomy is, though, not that distinct, as high self-esteem, personal control and sense of identity appear to improve subjective wellbeing for Eastern cultures as well as Western ones. Low self-esteem does not appear to be associated with wellbeing in any culture.

People in individualistic societies tend to report higher levels of happiness than people in collectivistic ones which are not accounted for by socioeconomic factors alone (Suh and Koo 2008). This may relate to collectivistic cultures emphasising the maintenance of social order and harmony leading to the expectation that members suppress their personal desires to promote collective interests. They value self-regulation over the self-expression and self-sufficiency highly prized in individualistic cultures.

Importance of place

With the globalisation of businesses contemporary societies are more blurred than they were in the past. Whilst this blurring is evident, anthropologists highlight the need to recognise a multiplicity of 'wellbeings' and suggest the importance of place or context should not be ignored (Mathews and Izquierdo 2009).

Atkinson *et al.* (2012: 8) identify that place is important; in studies of wellbeing it holds a "position as inherently relational in both its production and its influence". Place-making through relationships, activities, emotions and imaginations plays a significant role in people's sense of wellbeing. The importance of place has been identified by present day philosophers (Todres and Galvin 2010) as well as anthropologists. Anthropologists also indicate the need to consider non-human relationships alongside human relationships in the exploration of wellbeing. Sarmiento Barletti (2011), in his Ph.D study in the Peruvian Amazon, highlights the connection between wellbeing and human–non-human relations for the indigenous Ashaninka people. Their approach to living well is in pursuit of *kametsa asaiki*, 'living well together'. There is also evidence on social media of people having close attachments to animals, which are based on various links to wellbeing such as provision of needs, doing the right thing and happiness.

Religious wellbeing

Sixty per cent of the global population follow a religious system; the rest are atheist or have no established religion. The four most prevalent religions are: Christianity (2.4 billion followers), Islam (1.5 billion followers), Hinduism (900 million followers), Buddhism (380 million followers). However these numbers are problematic, particularly as atheists could be part of a Hindu or

Buddhist culture. The following four boxes offer an understanding of wellbeing from within each of these religious groups.

Box 2.1 Islamic cultural view of wellbeing

Islam as a religion has an influencing role in clarifying different key aspects of individuals' lives and shaping their way of living. However, the differences between Muslim scholars and communities in interpreting some teachings and practices of the religion and vast racial backgrounds of Muslims had a major role in shaping and maintaining various indigenous cultures. Culture has influenced understanding of wellbeing in two ways:

- The social heritage that is acquired from ancestors, which mainly formed understanding and a belief system about life, self, society and God.
- Conscious involvement in different societal and professional discussions that explore relevant aspects of wellbeing, such as health, happiness, quality of life and satisfaction.

The religion of Islam does not only focus on the relationship between an individual and God 'The Creator', but a style of life that consists of a comprehensive ideology about the wellbeing of individuals and societies. Through its Holy Book, the Quran, Islam reveals its rules that cover different aspects of life and urge Muslims 'believers' to follow certain guidelines to live a satisfying life. Moreover, Muslims consider the teachings and doings of Prophet Muhammed as an essential key to attain a lifelong wellbeing. Islam, through its Holy Book, enforces the value of it being a practice religion that connects its rules and laws to every aspect of a human's life that includes personal, social, spiritual and even political matters. The Quran uses different approaches to urge Muslims to have and maintain a satisfying life that is mainly achieved by following God's commands and guidelines, and it discourages them from any disobedience. Islam has a major role in devotees' understanding of wellbeing due to its deep philosophical underpinnings of life and strict religious practices.

Islam considers human beings as vicegerent of God on earth and that they hold a high position when compared to other creatures:

> Quran (2:30) "*And [mention, O Mohammed], when your Lord said to the Angels, 'Indeed, I will make upon the earth a successive authority.*' They said, '*Will You place upon it one who causes corruption therein and sheds blood, while we declare Your praise and sanctify You?*' Allah said, '*Indeed, I know that which you do not know.*'"

> Quran (17:70) "*And surely We have honoured the children of Adam, and We carry them in the land and the sea, and We have given them the good things, and We have made them to excel by an appropriate excellence over most of those whom We have created.*"

The Quran outlines that human beings are created in the best form that can support them in having a decent and/or satisfying life. It is believed that this is an important value that devotees gain from this religion as it indicates that humankind is created to be capable of adapting and developing.

> Quran (95:4) "*We have certainly created man in the best of stature.*"

In different instances, 'man' in the Quran is used to refer to both genders, men and women. The concept of existence and the aim to fulfil a higher purpose in life is another philosophical concept that promotes the Islamic perspective of wellbeing. God mentions in the Quran that the primary purpose for humankind in this universe is to worship and serve Him. Interestingly, the Quran promotes the ideology that worshipping God does not only entail believing in Him, but fulfilling one's internal and external life needs based on the guidelines/laws of God. It is believed that those laws outline the ways, standards and morals to have a happy and satisfying life in this world and the hereafter (Mawdudi 1961 and Nasr 2003).

> Quran (51:56) "*And I did not create the jinn and mankind except to worship Me.*"

Akhtar (2008) indicated that Islam is a law-centred religion that originates from correct conduct rather than solely from the right belief. This nature of Islam enforces the principle that human beings are capable of deciding for themselves and, thus, they are urged to behave correctly.

Islam teachings posit that God is the only perfect one and no human being is infallible. Guilt is considered an indication of individuals' awareness of committing a sin or a wrongful act, thought or intention, which may impact an individual's wellbeing if not properly corrected. Thus, Muslims are urged by Quranic teachings to repent their bad deeds and to do all they can to refrain from them. One of the names that the Quran reports for God is Al-Ghafoor (the most forgiving), indicating in 90 verses that all sinners are offered countless opportunities of repentance and redemption.

God states in the Quran (39:53), *"Say, 'O My servants who have transgressed against themselves (by sinning), do not despair of the mercy of Allah. Indeed, Allah forgives all sins. Indeed, it is He who is the Forgiving, the Merciful.'"* A whole chapter in the Quran is named 'The Repentance' that discusses the impacts of sins and commends believers to seek God's forgiveness to overcome guilt and regain the sense of wellbeing. The Quran (66:08) states, "*O ye who believe! Turn to God with sincere repentance, in the hope that your Lord will remove from you your ills and admit you to Gardens beneath which Rivers flow.*"

Box 2.2 Christian cultural view of wellbeing

Wellbeing does not at first sight appear to be a Christian concept, or at least not a biblical one. The two 'classic' English translations, the Authorised (King James) Version and Revised Standard Version do not contain the term at all. Neither do two 'literal' versions, Young's Literal Translation and the Disciples' Literal New Testament.

A popular modern translation, the New International Version (NIV), contains no occurrences in the New Testament, and only seven in the Old Testament. These translate several different Hebrew terms, the key one of which appears to be *shalom*. This word is typically translated as 'peace' but has a richer meaning than 'absence of war'. Various sources gloss it as *benefit, completeness, peace, peacetime, prosperity, welfare, well, wholeness*, or, indeed, '*wellbeing*'.

Being a Hebrew word, *shalom* does not occur in the Greek New Testament. If we look for 'peace', as the most common translation, we find 93 instances in NIV. Many of these are the conventional greeting 'Peace be with you' or the valediction 'Go in peace', or a greeting such as 'Grace and peace to you from God our Father and the Lord Jesus Christ' in the epistles. The Orthodox Jewish Bible (OJB) (an English translation aimed at Jewish people and using Hebrew/Jewish terms where appropriate) uses 'shalom' in all these instances.

Some other occurrences are as follows. The text is taken from the NIV, and 'peace' is given as 'shalom' in the OJB in all cases:

- Luke 19:41–43 "*As he approached Jerusalem and saw the city, he wept over it and said, 'If you, even you, had only known on this day what would bring you peace – but now it is hidden from your eyes. The days will come upon you when your enemies will build an embankment against you and encircle you and hem you in on every side.'*"
- John 14:27 "*Peace I leave with you; my peace I give you. I do not give to you as the world gives. Do not let your hearts be troubled and do not be afraid.*"
- John 16:33 "*I have told you these things, so that in me you may have peace. In this world you will have trouble. But take heart! I have overcome the world.*"
- Acts 10:36 "*You know the message God sent to the people of Israel, announcing the good news of peace through Jesus Christ, who is Lord of all.*"
- Romans 2:9–11 "*There will be trouble and distress for every human being who does evil: first for the Jew, then for the Gentile; but glory, honour and peace for everyone who does good: first for the Jew, then for the Gentile. For God does not show favouritism.*"
- Romans 8:6 "*The mind governed by the flesh is death, but the mind governed by the Spirit is life and peace.*"
- Romans 15:13 "*May the God of hope fill you with all joy and peace as you trust in him, so that you may overflow with hope by the power of the Holy Spirit.*"

- Galatians 5:22–23 "*But the fruit of the Spirit is love, joy, peace, forbearance, kindness, goodness, faithfulness, gentleness and self-control. Against such things there is no law.*"
- Philippians 4:6–8 "*Do not be anxious about anything, but in every situation, by prayer and petition, with thanksgiving, present your requests to God. And the peace of God, which transcends all understanding, will guard your hearts and your minds in Christ Jesus.*"
- 2 Thessalonians 3:16 "*Now may the Lord of peace himself give you peace at all times and in every way. The Lord be with all of you.*"
- 2 Timothy 2:22 "*Flee the evil desires of youth and pursue righteousness, faith, love and peace, along with those who call on the Lord out of a pure heart.*"
- Hebrews 12:11 "*No discipline seems pleasant at the time, but painful. Later on, however, it produces a harvest of righteousness and peace for those who have been trained by it.*"
- Hebrews 12:14 "*Make every effort to live in peace with everyone and to be holy; without holiness no one will see the Lord.*"
- 1 Peter 3:11 Quoting Psalm 34: "*[Whoever would love life and see good days] They must turn from evil and do good; they must seek peace and pursue it.*"

So, we have two main themes:

1 *Shalom* is a gift of God and/or Jesus, a result of the Holy Spirit in us.
2 *Shalom* is something to pursue, paired with turning from evil.

These need not be contradictory: Christians should choose to do right, whilst recognising that we can never be perfect; we must still accept God's gift of forgiveness and justification.

Wellbeing is generally defined as 'The state of being comfortable, healthy or happy'. The Christian would probably prefer to substitute 'joyful' for 'happy'. Happiness could be seen as somewhat superficial whilst joy is deeper-rooted. It is notable that many in the persecuted church, for example in totalitarian atheist or some Islamic countries, can maintain their joy despite a distinct lack of physical comfort and possibly ill health brought about by their living conditions. This reflects the experience of the apostle Paul, who states,

> I know what it is to be in need, and I know what it is to have plenty. I have learned the secret of being content in any and every situation, whether well fed or hungry, whether living in plenty or in want.
>
> (Philippians 4:12)

One factor influencing one's joy (or happiness) is guilt: a person aware of their guilt will have diminished wellbeing. In Christian belief, Jesus has died on our behalf, paying the penalty for all wrong-doing and leaving us free of guilt, if we accept that offer. This leads to a second factor: unforgiveness of others by ourselves. A person carrying long-term resentment of others also has diminished wellbeing. As a result of God's forgiveness of us, Christians are both required to forgive others and enabled or strengthened to do so.

Christians look forward to the kingdom of God being established on the earth. This will result in peace, justice, righteousness, plenty and so on, in wellbeing in fact. In the meantime, however, we inevitably experience conflict, injustice, etc. but can maintain our wellbeing through confidence in Jesus Christ.

Box 2.3 Buddhist cultural view of wellbeing

Buddhism was founded by Goutam Buddha who wandered experiencing many cultures and religions over 2500 years ago but became disillusioned with them all. During this period and through meditation he came to believe that nothing in the world is permanent and everyone will experience suffering, leading to Buddhists accepting three universal truths and four noble truths about life.

Three universal truths

1. Everything in life is impermanent and always changing.
2. Because nothing is permanent a life based on possessions does not make you happy.
3. There is no eternal unchanging soul and self; a person is just a collection of changing characteristics or attributes.

Four noble truths

1. Human life involves a lot of suffering.
2. The cause of suffering is greed.
3. There is an end to suffering.
4. The way to end suffering is to follow the middle path.

Buddha recommended the middle path as the way to achieve nirvana, quenching or extinguishing, a transcendence from suffering. Nirvana is characterised by peace and deep spiritual joy. The middle path is one of not leading a life of luxury and indulgence but also not one of too much fasting and hardship. This path has eight guiding principles:

1. Right understanding and viewpoint (based on the Four Noble Truths).
2. Right values and attitude (compassion rather than selfishness).
3. Right speech (don't tell lies, avoid harsh, abusive speech, avoid gossip).
4. Right action (help others, live honestly, don't harm living things, take care of the environment).

5 Right work (do something useful, avoid jobs which harm others).
6 Right effort (encourage good, helpful thoughts, discourage unwholesome destructive thoughts).
7 Right mindfulness (be aware of what you feel, think and do).
8 Right meditation (calm mind, practise meditation which leads to nirvana) (O'Brien 2019).

Buddhists acknowledge the interdependence of mind and body, accepting that emotions and thoughts impact on wellbeing. Accordingly, the mind is powerful and can control many bodily functions. This leads to promotion of mind–body approaches to health and wellbeing but also highlights the complex interaction between the embodied person and their environment. A sense of purpose, a meaning to life facilitates living longer, healthier lives with compassion, generosity and patience making people strong and resilient. Belief incorporates working towards training the mind to understand and cultivate happiness through managing emotional states increasing loving kindness, compassion and sympathetic joy whilst reducing negative emotions to improve personal and societal wellbeing.

Ajahn Candasiri, a senior nun at the Amaravati Buddhist Monastery in Hertfordshire, states,

> In practice, I have found the process to be one of attuning, of attending carefully to what is happening within – sensing when there is ease, harmony; knowing also when one's view is at odds with What Is. I find that the images that Jesus uses to describe the Kingdom of Heaven explain this well. It is like a seed that under favourable conditions germinates and grows into a tree. We ourselves create the conditions that either promote wellbeing and the growth of understanding, or cause harm to ourselves or others. We don't need a God to consign us to the nether regions of some hell realm if we are foolish or selfish – it happens naturally. Similarly, when we fill our lives with goodness, we feel happy – that's a heavenly state".
>
> (2014)

Box 2.4 Hinduist cultural view of wellbeing

Hinduism encompasses great diversity in beliefs and practices but has a shared world view, a set of metaphysical and philosophical concepts to life and the world. Whilst Hinduism is acknowledged as having many manifestations of God, the religious leaders state that there is one God that is looked at in different ways. The general name for God in Hinduism is Brahman (external) and the name of the divine essence within us is Atman (internal). Internal and external divinity are one and the same, infinite and eternal. However, God is also present in all creation. Orthodox Hindus usually base their values, beliefs and practices on the writings in the Veda. The Veda is made up of four parts and each of these also has four parts.

- **The Samhitas** are the most ancient part of the Vedas, consisting of hymns of praise to God.
- **The Brahmanas** are rituals and prayers to guide the priests in their duties.
- **The Aranyakas** concern worship and meditation.
- **The Upanishads** consist of the mystical and philosophical teachings of Hinduism.

The fundamental, metaphysical teaching of Hinduism (Vedanta) is that a human being's basic nature is not confined to the body or the mind. Hinduism offers the sense of the divine spirit within the person, the spark of God within the soul, but this also resides in the whole of creation. This pure divine spirit is full of peace, joy and wisdom. It unites the person and the rest of creation with God and can be experienced through yoga, a linking of inner self with inner spirit. There are four types of yoga which offer the route to experiencing God for different human temperaments; Karma (discipline seeking), Bhakti (presence seeking), Jnana (seeking clarity of sight), Raja (inner divinity seeking). This presents wellbeing as a vision of health and happiness.

Hinduism offers a code of behaviour for its adherents called Dharma. Appropriate behaviour or duties are determined by a person's social position (Varma). There are four main social positions: Brahmins (priests and teachers), Kshatriyas (rulers and soldiers), Vaishyas (merchants) and Shudras (workers).

Menon (2012) undertook her doctoral studies exploring the meaning of happiness and wellbeing for Hindu women in a temple town in Oriya. The women did not believe that adults could gain happiness, but that wellbeing was more achievable. They shared that happiness could only be experienced by children as they were unaware of the burdens of life. Adults would only ever be able to experience happiness fleetingly as they were aware of the burdens and suffering. The experience of wellbeing for these women was dependent on their life stage but also their social position. Given this context mature adulthood appeared to have the most opportunity for women to experience wellbeing. For Oriya Hindu women this is when they are most dominant in their households and they feel morally and emotionally coherent. This is their cultural model of wellbeing.

A cultural view of wellbeing based on faith

Many societies describe themselves as belonging to one of the Christian religious groups, the largest religious group globally. This, though, has a wide variety of meanings; it may mean they live their lives according to the Bible as interpreted by their priest or minister or just that they hope to go to heaven when they die. In the US, Africa and Europe Christians may label themselves as 'practising' which usually infers they are actively engaged in some form of worship as opposed to Christian by birth. Other terms are also used such as 'born again'. Within the Christian family there are three main categories: Catholic, Protestant and Orthodox with numerous denominations (Greek Orthodox, Russian Orthodox, Aramaic, Presbyterian, Baptist, Pentecostal, Anglican etc.) each of which focuses on different parts of the message and has different ritualistic behaviours.

Islam meanwhile has two main groups, the Sunni and Shi'ite Muslims, mostly due to a lack of successor for Mohammed, but there are numerous smaller groups who focus on individual scholars of Islam. Buddhism too has two main types, Theravada and Mahayana, but Mahayana also has three branches. Meanwhile Hindus could be said to have thousands of approaches.

Jews, Muslims and Christians all worship the one and only God for whom shalom is essential for wellbeing. Christians believe Jesus was the son of God and died to save them from their sins and Muslims accept Jesus as a prophet, but the prophet Mohammed is acknowledged as the most significant and recent to provide God's message. Hindus can also be said to have one God. The Hindu God resides within and alongside people, is everywhere in everything and not a distinct separate being. Each person can have their own God but each is part of the whole God. Buddhists, though, do not acknowledge any divine entity.

Whilst shalom is key to wellbeing for Jews, Christians and Muslims and influenced by God, for Buddhists happiness is key which is the individual's responsibility and within their control. For Hindus personal responsibility and control are also dictators of their destiny as Karma leads to the person experiencing in their next life the consequences of behaviour in their current incarnation.

In conclusion

Mental wellbeing is an important part of both psychological and physical health. Research has found that mental wellbeing can have a distinct impact on improving physical health and reducing mortality (HM Gov. 2010). It is not the number of negative or positive experiences per se that influence mental wellbeing. It is how they are perceived; it is the meaning given to them. Interpersonal relationships moderate the effect of life events; higher levels of quality of interpersonal relationships lead to a greater sense of wellbeing (Burns and Machin 2013).

Mental wellbeing has been described by Keyes and Seligman (positive psychologists) as *flourishing*, which they state is a new and dynamic approach. They state flourishing is reaching one's potential which is the same definition humanists offer. Whilst their goal is the same, Keyes and Seligman propose a complex explanation of how this is achieved, either through Seligman's five domains (PERMA) or Keyes' three dimensions (social, psychological and emotional wellbeing). The Office for National Statistics (2013) gives ten domains and forty-one elements. These domains and dimensions provide models for scientific researchers to measure and explore but they reduce human experiences.

Philosophically, anthropologically and psychologically the key to understanding wellbeing is through the experience of joy mediated by the body, truth, beauty and/or the divine; this makes suffering in life experiences meaningful and worthwhile.

References

Atkinson, S., Fuller, S., Painter, J. (Eds.) 2012. *Wellbeing and Place*. Farnham: Ashgate.

Barker, S. 2013. *Caring for Older People in Nursing*. Exeter: Learning Matters.

Barker, S. 2016. *Psychology for Nurses and Health Care Practitioners to Support Compassionate Care*. London: Sage.

Bentham, J. 2018 [1789]. *Utilitarianism: Introduction to the Principles of Morals and Legislation* (classic reprint). Bibliobazaar, p. 11.

Burns, R.A., Machin, M.A. 2013. "Psychological Wellbeing and the Diathesis Stress Hypothesis Model: The Role of Psychological Functioning and Quality of Relations in Promoting Subjective Well-being in a Life Events Study", *Personality and Individual Differences*, 54, 3, 321–326.

Candasiri, A. 2014. Jesus Through Buddhist Eyes. www.bbc.co.uk/religion/religions/buddhism/beliefs/jesusandbuddhism_1.shtml.

Cope, A., 2017. "With Mental Health Problems on the Rise in Classrooms, We're Bringing Happiness Inspectors into Schools and Developing a GCSE in Wellbeing", *Guardian*, August 25, www.theguardian.com/teacher-network/2017/aug/25/childrens-mental-health-its-time-to-put-wellbeing-on-the-curriculum.

Department of Health (DoH). 2007. Commissioning Framework for Health and Well-being, p. 99. www.visionuk.org.uk/download/archive_1/pdf/PDF%20health%20and%20well(1).pdf

Diener, E., Suh, E. 1997. "Measuring Quality of Life: Economic, Social, and Subjective Indicators", *Social Indicators Research*, 40, 1–2, 189–216. DOI: http://dx.doi.org/10.1023/A:1006859511756.

Dodge, R., Daly, A., Huyton, J., Sanders, L. 2012. "The Challenge of Defining Wellbeing", *International Journal of Wellbeing*, 2, 3, 222–235.

Ferraro, E., Sarmiento Barletti, J.P. 2016. "Placing Wellbeing Anthropological Perspectives on Wellbeing and Place", *Anthropology in Action*, 23, 3 (Winter 2016), 1–5.

Gov UK. 2014. Wellbeing. Why It Matters to Health Policy. https://assets.publishing.service.gov.uk/government/uploads/system/uploads/attachment_data/file/277566/Narrative__January_2014_.pdf.

Gov. UK. 2017a. Ten Facts That Sum Our Nation's Health in 2017. https://publichealthmatters.blog.gov.uk/2017/07/13/10-facts-that-sum-up-our-nations-health-in-2017/.

Gov. UK. 2017b. What's Happening with Mortality Rates in England? https://publichealthmatters.blog.gov.uk/2017/07/20/whats-happening-with-mortality-rates-in-england/.

Herbert, S. 2000. "For Ethnography", *Progress in Human Geography*, 24, 4, 550–568.

HM Gov. 2010. Health and Wellbeing Today. https://assets.publishing.service.gov.uk/government/uploads/system/uploads/attachment_data/file/215911/dh_122238.pdf.

James, W. 1988 [1902]. *Writings 1902–1910*. New York: Library of America.

Keyes, C.L.M. 2002. "The Mental Health Continuum: From Languishing to Flourishing in Life", *Journal of Health and Social Behavior*, 43, 2, 207–222.

Lake, E. 2018. "Know Yourself. What Is Mindfulness", *Sun*, 26 July, www.thesun.co.uk/fabulous/4100076/mindfulness-colouring-books-meditation-exercise-mental-wellbeing-practice/.

Mathews, G., Izquierdo, C. (Eds.) 2009. *Pursuits of Happiness: Well-being in Anthropological Perspective*. New York: Berghahn.

Menon, U. 2012. "Hinduism, Happiness and Wellbeing: A Case Study of Adulthood in an Oriya Hindu Temple Town". Available from: www.researchgate.net/publication/279409932_[accessed April 25 2019].

Morrow, V., Mayall, B. 2009. "What Is Wrong with Children's Wellbeing in the UK? Questions of Meaning and Measurement", *Journal of Social Welfare and Family Law*, 31, 3, 217–229.

O'Brien, B. 2019. The Eightfold Path: The Way to Enlightenment in Buddhism. Available at: www.learnreligions.com/the-eightfold-path-450067.

Office for National Statistics (ONS). 2013. Measuring What Matters: Understanding the Nation's Wellbeing. Available at: www.ons.gov.uk/ons/interactive/well-being-wheel-of-measures/index.html.

Pawelski, J.O. 2003. "William James, Positive Psychology, and Healthy-Mindedness", *The Journal of Speculative Philosophy*, 17, 1, 53–67. DOI:10.1353/jsp. 2003.0025.

Rogers, C.R. 1961. *On Becoming a Person: A Therapist's View of Psychotherapy*. London: Constable, p. 186.

Ryff, C.D. 1989. "Happiness Is Everything, or Is It? Explorations on the Meaning of Psychological Wellbeing", *Journal of Personality and Social Psychology*, 57, 1069–1081. DOI: http://dx.doi.org/10.1037/00223514.57.6.1069.

Ryff, C., Singer, B. 2008. "Know Thyself and Become What You Are: An Eudaimonic Approach to Psychological Wellbeing", *Journal of Happiness Studies*, 9, 13–39. DOI: http://dx.doi.org/10.1007/s10902-0069019.

Sarmiento Barletti, J.P. 2011. Kametsa Asaiki: The Pursuit of the "Good Life" in an Ashaninka Village (Peruvian Amazonia). https://core.ac.uk/display/1586689.

Seligman, M.E.P. 1998. "The President's Address", *American Psychologist*, 54, 559–562.

Seligman, M.E.P. 2011. *Flourish – A New Understanding of Happiness and Well-being – and How to Achieve Them*. London: Nicholas Brealey Publishing.

Social Care Institute for Excellence (SCIE). 2005. Update for SCIE Best Practice Guide, Assessing the Mental Health Needs of Older People. www.scie.org.uk/publications/guides/guide03/files/research.pdf?res=true

Suh, E.M., Koo, J. 2008. "Comparing Subjective Well-being Across Cultures and Nations: The 'What' and 'Why' Questions". *In*: Eid, M. and Larsen, R.J. (Eds.) *The Science of Subjective Well-Being*. New York: Guilford Press, pp. 414–430.

Thomas, J. 2009. Working Paper: Current Measures and the Challenges of Measuring Children's Wellbeing. Newport: Office for National Statistics.

Todres, L., Galvin, K. 2010. "'Dwelling-mobility': An Existential Theory of Well-being", *International Journal of Qualitative Studies on Health and Well-being*, 5, 3. DOI: 10.3402/qhw.v5i3.5444.

Chapter 3

Embodied subjective self and resilience

Introduction

In Chapter 2, wellbeing was explored from a psychological, philosophical and anthropological perspective, where it was established that wellbeing had subjective and objective dimensions. An examination of self can also derive a definition proposing these two dimensions. As with wellbeing the objective self, that which can be measured and observed by others, also labelled self-concept or personality, is limited and can reduce understanding of the rich diverse experience of being a person. Within this chapter there is acknowledgement of a psychological understanding of the self objectively, but its primary focus is on the subjective, embodied experiences of the self, incorporating the intuitive, spiritual soul of the person.

Initially in this chapter there will be a consideration of what is understood of the objective self or social theories of self, followed by embodiment and how this relates to personal experiences. The chapter will be completed by exploring subjective self in more detail and finish with how people may manage their subjective wellbeing through self-knowledge and resilience.

Social theories of self

Behaviourism

According to behaviourists people start learning from birth; they are born with the ability to learn, and continue to learn throughout their lives. It is this behaviour that demonstrates the personality of the individual; people learn to be who they are.

The founder of behaviourism, John B. Watson (1878–1958), indicated the individual self can only be ascertained by observing their behaviour – it is a person's behaviour that determines who they are. Philosophically behaviourism accepts the concept that people are born as a *'tabula rasa'*. This is based on John Locke's (1632–1704) expression of the idea in his *Essay Concerning Human Understanding* but the concept can be tracked back to Aristotle through the likes of Persian philosopher Avicenna (Ibn Sina in Arabic) in the eleventh century.

Adopting this philosophical concept and using a traditional natural sciences approach, Watson undertook research on stimulus-response procedures through which he developed the scientific concept of *classical conditioning* or learning by association. This is a form of reflexive learning where reflexive responses can be trained by being paired with a stimulus. The most famous demonstration of this was the salivating dogs experiment of Ivan Pavlov (1849–1936). Given the theory of classical conditioning, the person does not need conscious awareness or need to make choices about their behaviour; they reflexively learn to behave in certain ways due to stimuli being paired, for example the 'little Albert' experiment (see Box 3.1).

In the 1930s B.F. Skinner extended behaviourism to individual experiences such as thoughts and feelings, stating they should be explored using a natural (traditional) sciences approach just as previous behaviourists had with explicitly observable behaviours. He was particularly interested in the controlling nature of the environment, including other people, and developed the theory of learning called *operant conditioning*. Operant conditioning is learning through *reinforcement*. Behaviour that is adaptive or socially acceptable is reinforced through rewards in the environment. When a person is rewarded, they are more likely to repeat the behaviour and if behaviour is punished they are less likely to repeat it.

These early behaviourists had problems accounting for novel responses leading to new theories of human behaviour. These were achieved through the work of researchers such as Albert Bandura who established the *social learning theory*. Bandura suggested that personality emerges from the interaction between thoughts, the environment and behaviour through:

- Observational learning
- Reinforcement
- Punishment

Bandura, whilst accepting the learning processes of classical (Watson and Pavlov) and operant (Skinner) conditioning, identified through his studies

Box 3.1 Little Albert study (Watson and Raynor 1920)

The study involved an eleven-month-old boy, who was called Albert. Albert showed no fear of white furry creatures such as rats and rabbits, just curiosity, but he did respond fearfully and cry when a loud noise was made. After a number of pairings where the noise and white furry animals were presented together Albert responded fearfully when a white furry animal was presented alone. Albert had been classically conditioned to fearfully respond to these innocuous animals.

Box 3.2 Bobo doll experiment

In 1961 and 1963 Albert Bandura developed empirical experiments to test his theory that children learn behaviour such as aggression. He set up experiments where children were observed playing with a number of toys including a 'bobo doll', an inflatable doll weighted at the bottom so that when knocked it does not fall over. When children were given a 'bobo doll' to play with they did not undertake any aggressive play but after they had observed an adult (role model) being aggressive towards the doll they imitated this behaviour (Barker 2016).

(such as the Bobo doll experiments in 1965; see Box 3.2) that people learnt and changed their behaviour through observation and imitation as well. They learn vicariously through observing what responses occur to others' behaviour; these others are people called *role models*. He acknowledged that some role models were more effective than others, for example role models that were socially accepted were rewarded and those similar in some way to the observer were more likely to be imitated.

Through the process of observation and imitation called *modelling* children develop a self-concept and self-efficacy which are strengthened in adulthood.

Self-concept – a collection of thoughts or ideas about oneself, for example 'I am a caring person'.

Self-efficacy – the belief in one's own ability to achieve a goal, for example 'I can ride a bike'.

Modelling allows the person to gain attitudes, values and the ability to self-evaluate, which in turn facilitates the person's ability to function in their society. This is seen as the person internalising social standards and expectations. Bandura based his theory on a belief in '*reciprocal determinism*'; behaviour can be determined or expected through internalised mutual understanding: 'If I behave like this you should behave like that'.

For many there is an assumption that behaviourism is a collection of theories that were relevant to the twentieth century but have limited use in the twenty-first century. This, though, is unfounded especially in the educational and mental health arenas. Johnson (2015: 137) clearly outlines the importance of behavioural analysis in the classroom, stating, "Recent neuroscientific research in embodied and embedded cognition supports the radical behavioural position". The journal *Behavior Therapy* also offers a wealth of studies which use behaviourism in the development of wellbeing, for example O'Mahen *et al.* (2019).

Symbolic interaction theory

Symbolic interaction offers a method for exploring how individuals actively understand their social reality and themselves by interacting with others. Its

> **Box 3.3 Reich *et al.*'s (2018) SIT experiment**
>
> Reich *et al.* undertook a study to explore symbolic interactions; the symbols in this case were the 'Like' icons on social networking sites and how these impacted on the participants' sense of inclusion or exclusion. The participants, Facebook users, wrote a small update on what they had been doing and were then given hypothetical feedback on the number of Likes they received (0, 2, or 30) and who (close friends or acquaintances) pressed the Like button. Statistical analysis demonstrated that belongingness and self-esteem needs are threatened when people do not receive Likes. The number of Likes received directly affected their self-evaluation regardless of who had 'clicked' on the Like icon.

founder, George Herbert Mead (1863–1931), was a social scientist and pragmatic philosopher. He believed that people are unable to know the world without being part of it; the two are intrinsically linked.

For Mead, social reality was not stable; it is in a state of continuous flux, always changing, leading to the need for people to construct and reconstruct meaning in their social lives through interacting with other people. In this construction people use symbols such as language (spoken or written) and non-verbal gestures. This facilitates an understanding of the self through observation and facilitates measurement. Whilst interactionists tend to rely on observational or ethnographic studies some use surveys, interviews and experiments.

In their social constructions, people take on roles, so unlike behaviourism where the person is said to be controlled by the environment or others, the person here is a co-creator in developing social reality. Whilst being co-creators, individuals will not necessarily have equal power within their interactions, leading to numerous social emotional experiences being promulgated or extinguished such as shame and pride.

Social Interaction Theory (SIT) remains a popular method for understanding how people develop their self-concept. For example, the recent articles by Waldbuesser (2019) teaching university students and Reich *et al.* (2018) exploring symbolic interactions and need satisfaction online (see Box 3.3).

A number of newer theories have their foundation in symbolic interactionism, such as:

Erving Goffman's dramaturgy

Erving Goffman (1922–1982) used his understanding of SIT to develop his *dramaturgy* theory which suggests people are only the roles they are playing in the moment. This was articulately expressed in his first and most well-known book, *The Presentation of Self in Everyday Life* (1959). Within this book Goffman states that personal interactions are a sort of '*information game*'. In this 'game' each individual attempts to control how their actions are being perceived but at the same time tries to understand the real meaning of their interactional partner. People are undertaking *impression management* as part of their acting and at the same time observing and interrogating the other person's concealed facts and motives. This is achieved through observing less well-hidden behaviours such as eye contact, language fluidity and hesitations (McCoy 2017).

Key concepts in Goffman's theory are impression management, face work (attempting to maintain personal [face] integrity), avoidance processes (behaviours undertaken to reduce the risk of loss of face) and corrective processes (behaviours to restore face integrity). This all takes place on the 'stage' or '*front*'. For Goffman this has three important features: the setting, appearance and manner. Setting and management of appearance can be constructed by each actor with negotiation (SIT) but manner (the way a person walks, talks, holds themselves) may take a deeper form of acting (Hochschild 1983).

Personality or self-concept defined from a cognitive and scientific psychological perspective could be defined as the relatively stable traits or characteristics demonstrated by a person over time and in different situations (Barker 2016). Given Goffman's identification that people may have concealed facts and motives alongside the concept of manner, these might indicate stable traits of the person fulfilling the definition. This is despite his indication that people are purely role actors.

Cooley's 'looking glass self'

The term 'the looking glass self' was coined by Charles Horton Cooley in 1902 and refers to developing a self-concept through viewing one's self in a mirror using SIT. It is where a person imagines how another person may perceive them. This theory states that each person perceives other individuals in a unique way. For example, if a young person looks in the metaphorical mirror, they could imagine how their mother would perceive them, perhaps as young, foolish and loveable. If the same young person imagines how one of their peers perceives them, it might be quite different. These different perspectives coalesce in the individual's perception to form their self-concept, fulfilling the cognitive definition of personality, but unlike Goffman offer a more emotive element.

Cooley provides the following process to self-identification:

1. We imagine how we must appear before others.
2. We imagine and react to what we feel about the judgements about our appearance.
3. We develop our self through the judgement of others.

(Siljanovska and Stojcevska 2018: 63)

Siljanovska and Stojcevska (2018) offer a critical analysis of this theory in modern times and whilst they identify there is evidence to support people changing themselves due to their perception of other's views, they also identify that the person in virtual reality can offer a self-presentation that does not involve a change of self-concept. They also argue that this theory contrasts with Roger's humanistic theory which will be explored later.

Social comparison theory

Leon Festinger (1954) offered another social theory of self-concept called social comparison theory. He stated that people are driven to gain accurate '*self-evaluation*' in a similar manner to Bandura's social learning theory. For Festinger this is where people evaluate themselves, their opinions, knowledge and abilities by comparing themselves with others. Through self-evaluation people can then establish their self-concept or self-definition, their enduring traits.

Festinger conceptualised social comparison (referred to as the classical perspective in social comparison) as a deliberate process, not one in which individuals automatically compare themselves to others. There have been a number of reviews of this theory, for example Mussweiler (2003), Suls *et al.* (2002) and Guimond (2006). More recent research has indicated that social comparison can be automatic, operating at a spontaneous level without intention or control. Within this type of comparison theory (the modern perspective) there are two processes; the first is automatic comparison and the second is controlled and occurs after the initial comparison has been made (Chatard *et al.* 2017). This subliminal social comparison has been found to be an effective form of self-evaluation (Chatard *et al.* 2017).

Summary of social theories of self

There are many social theories of the self, identified as self-concept or personality. Here just a few of the most popular ones have been explored. All these social psychological understandings of the self have their foundations in the behavioural perspective. Therefore they all involve some level of learning with the later and more cognitive theories still including classical, operant and social learning. These cognitive theories (SIT, dramaturgical, looking glass self, social comparison) also involve observation of self and others leading to self-evaluation and management. They support a cognitive psychological definition of personality: the relatively stable traits or characteristics demonstrated by a person over time.

Selfhood

The concept of personal selfhood or complete autonomy is widely accepted in Western societies, incorporating both objective and subjective models of self, particularly when considering mental wellbeing. This has been criticised for its impact on racial, sexual and national divides due to its exclusion of self-in-others and others-in-self. The premise of the independent self within an individualist society facilitates a simple but impaired judicial system where there is a great divide in acquisitions and wealth. The individual is subliminally accepted as responsible for their situation with those who accumulate wealth seen as having made good choices, behaved well, and those who do not receiving some sort of punishment.

In contrast a society where selfhood is denied, which recognises the impact of others on individual behaviour and provides an expectation people will act altruistically for the needs of the community, can reduce the possibilities of the person achieving their potential. It may appear more just to share wealth and acquisitions but politically this is a difficult society to manage within current globalisation. Whilst scientists explore behaviour of groups and individuals it is important to recognise there are ways of understanding personhood other than the cognitive behavioural one.

Subjective self

Subjective self: my personal understanding of who I am.

Psychodynamic psychology

The cognitive psychological definition of self-concept or personality, the relatively stable traits or characteristics demonstrated by a person over time, is adequate for a cognitive behavioural perspective of the person and amenable to measurement but there are other perspectives. Psychologically the psychodynamic perspective of Sigmund Freud has had a huge impact on Western societies. This has been through his promotion of an unconscious part of the self, mental defence mechanisms, the structure of the personality and general usage of '*Freudian slips', parapraxes*.

Freud was one of the great thinkers of the twentieth century. He was influenced by the prevailing socio-political environment of his time, but he still had something to offer in exploration of the subjective self. The term psychodynamic implies that active forces within the personality motivate behaviour particularly between the three component parts of the personality or psyche. These three component parts are the *id*, *ego* and *superego*. The id and the superego are largely unconscious, and the ego is largely conscious (with some preconscious and unconscious components). As with an iceberg, most of the personality lies beneath the surface and therefore cannot be seen (Barker 2016).

Freud did not develop the concept of the unconscious; unconscious aspects of mentality were referred to as far back as the Hindu texts between 2500 and 600 BCE, but it was originally coined by Friedrich Schelling, an eighteenth century philosopher. It came into English awareness through the poet Samuel Coleridge, but Freud popularised and applied a structure to the term.

Freud offers an understanding that personality is *dynamic*: it is always in the process of changing and there are some parts of self that people will never be able to know; they are unconscious. Whilst this appears the same as the social theories of self his explanation of this instability of self is different. He states that the self, the personality, is always in conflict, this is between the id and superego which is continually being balanced by the ego.

This has implications for self-awareness; a psychodynamic perspective identifies that a person cannot know what is in their unconscious mind therefore a person can never have total knowledge of their self. Luft and Ingham (1955) developed a model which outlines four quadrants of self-awareness called the Johari window. This model indicates that there are parts of the mind that are private and others that are social or public but there is also a part of the self that cannot be seen by self or others. This is the unconscious part of the self. This means the total self cannot be scientifically measured by either self-report (introspection) or through observation. Understanding the behaviours of others can only be achieved psychodynamically through interpretation of overt behaviour and small windows into the mind such as dreams, free association and parapraxes (Freudian slips).

A psychodynamic perspective, alongside cognitive behavioural theories, offers differing prisms through which to view the self but psychology offers yet further perspectives.

Humanistic psychology

The humanistic psychologists identify themselves as the third force in psychology, their theories building on the philosophies and theories of both cognitive behaviourists and psychodynamic theorists. They accept that a person's self, their personality, develops and grows by learning and cognitive processing through their relationships initially with their early care givers and later in social interactions. The founding fathers of humanistic psychology were Carl Ransom Rogers (1902–1987) and Abraham Maslow (1908–1970).

The humanistic perspective is not one organised theory, but whilst differing in focus the theories are all based on the philosophical ideas of phenomenology particularly existentialism.

Philosophical foundations

Existential philosophers hold the premise that individuals are unique, aware of their lifeworld experiences, their experiences are within their personal control, people are free to make their own choices, and are responsible for their own existence. This philosophy underpins humanistic theories and humanistic philosophy.

> The Principles of Humanistic Philosophy:
>
> - Each person has control over their behaviour and experiences
> - People are aware of their own lifeworld experiences
> - On the path to self-actualisation the person is always in the process of becoming something different
> - Each person has the responsibility to realise their own potential
> - People who refuse to become will not realise the full possibilities of human existence
> - Consciousness, subjective feelings, moods and personal experiences are crucial because they all relate to one's existence in the world
>
> (Barker 2016: 159)

This philosophy underpins all the humanistic theories. Whilst Maslow was considered the first humanistic psychologist the leading proponent of this approach was Rogers. Rogers, as with the other humanistic psychologists, was influenced by theorists such as Freud, Thorndike and Dewey but he was also influenced by his own childhood deprivation.

Carl Ransom Rogers (1902–1987)

Rogers developed a therapy called client-centred therapy that was later to be recognised as person-centred therapy based on his underlying theory of the person. Rogers' assumptions about the person were:

> - Each person has their own sense of reality which is called their *phenomenological field* which develops through their experiences of the world.
> - Each person has a *self-actualising tendency* which motivates them to achieve their potential: *self-actualisation*.
> - Each person is continually undergoing an *organismic valuing process* – placing more value on experiences that move them towards self-actualisation.
>
> (Barker 2016)

Rogers identified that people could maintain their wellbeing by understanding themselves and working towards their unique potential. The view a person has of themselves, according to Rogers, could be *congruent* or *incongruent*. An incongruent self-concept is based on *conditions of worth* rather than an *organismic valuing process*. Conditions of worth are where people place a higher value on achieving positive regard from others rather than the attainment of personal potential, *self-actualisation. Positive regard* is necessary for a congruent self-concept but to strive for this can devalue it as it needs to be *unconditional.* Despite the problems of actively seeking positive regard the person, through a process of *subception* and *defence*, protects incongruence and prevents change (Rogers 1951), which has some similarity with Freud's mental defence mechanisms. These are where the person provides explanations and rationales for why it is important to do things to please others and gain their positive regard, rather than undertaking activities that would facilitate personal achievement of their potential.

As with Freud's mental defence mechanisms this is mostly done at a subconscious level but unlike Freud, Rogers states that the person is able, under the right conditions, to recognise subception and defences. They can then identify their potential and work towards it. Rogers (1957) states the '*necessary and sufficient*' conditions for the person to develop their wellbeing (become the person they are meant to be) as:

1 Therapist–client psychological contact
2 Client incongruence
3 Therapist congruence, or genuineness
4 Therapist has unconditional positive regard for client
5 Therapist demonstrates empathic understanding
6 Client perception

Rogers believed that a person could be facilitated to become themselves through the experience of non-judgemental positive regard which can be likened to the love shown to a child by its parents. If a child or adult does not receive this, they are likely to develop an incongruent sense of self and lack mental wellbeing.

Abraham Maslow (1908–1970)

Maslow was, as already identified, one of the first of the humanist psychologists. He developed a hierarchy of needs, which offers a framework for exploring individual motivation. Maslow believed that people need to be self-aware and that the ability to come to terms with one's self is necessary for psychological wellbeing. He suggested that behaviour could be understood in terms of the person seeking to fulfil personal goals to achieve a rewarding life.

Maslow's hierarchy puts physical and safety needs at the bottom as they need to be achieved first. The bottom needs of the triangular hierarchy are fulfilled through the person's deficiency drive. If they are not achieved the person will become unwell. The top part of the triangle highlights growth needs including love and belonging and aesthetic needs with self-actualisation at the very top. A person is always moving up the hierarchy as self-actualisation is not a permanent state and the person needs to continually fulfil the lower levels.

The earlier definition given of the self or personality was from a cognitive behavioural psychological perspective – personality is the relatively stable traits or characteristics demonstrated by a person over time. A more humanistic, person-centred psychological definition of personality could be: *it is the interaction between an individual's 'felt sense' which provides meaning through embodied relational knowing and the world in which the person lives in time and space.* This will be referred to again later in the book. In this definition there is no mention of traits or characteristics; it is focused on an intuitive knowing (see Chapter 1 for ways of knowing) from all the person's lived experiences. The self is a personal interpretation of one's unique relationship with their body (senses), mind (psychology/philosophy), soul (spirituality), others (people) and their world in time and space.

Embodiment

Embodied or embodiment is a concept that has differing definitions. It can be defined as the incarnation or personification of a concept or idea. However, within philosophy and psychology it has also been recognised as the way the body shapes the mind, ideas forming through bodily experiences. Its definition can be further extended to embodied knowledge. This is where the physical body understands something through bodily experiences or knows how to behave without conscious thought (intuitively) (Barker 2018).

Whether people can transcend their bodies created a divergence in phenomenological philosophy with Edmund Husserl (1859–1938), the founding father of phenomenology, and his student Heidegger having differing beliefs. Husserl believed that phenomenon could be intuited a priori to consciousness through *transcendental phenomenological reduction.* This would allow '*the ideal thing*' or '*the thing itself*' to be described before it was transformed by the mind, whereas Martin Heidegger (1989–1976), Husserl's student and successor, believed people could not distance themselves from their lifeworld or *dasein* (being there). Husserl's philosophical approach is established as epistemological whereas Heidegger's as ontological. Husserl offers a window into knowledge and understanding whereas Heidegger offers a window into a person's life, their experience of being. Heidegger states in his book *Being and Time* that being is time. To understand one's self the person needs to accept their life is finite; they are a temporal being.

Eugene Gendlin (1926–2017) and Les Todres (2007), from the same philosophical tradition, went further and wrote that all lifeworld experiences are embodied regardless of whether or not they could be intuited a priori. For Gendlin and Todres a subjective sense of self is embodied. Gendlin, despite being a philosopher, was a student of Rogers, the humanist psychologist and founder of client-centred therapy. From his collaboration with Rogers, Gendlin developed a process called 'focusing' (see Chapter 8), a method for paying attention to one's own body. This process facilitated Gendlin's exploration of the extent to which people used their '*felt sense*' in their daily lives.

Felt sense is different from emotional feelings; it is more a bodily awareness of living and ongoing life processes. Felt sense is a living interaction with the world. The more people are in tune with their felt sense, their experience of being alive in the world, the greater their opportunity for wellbeing. Felt sense can be developed through focusing.

Focusing is a process of becoming more attuned to bodily experiences, of being alive. It is about changing a vague sense of something to creating words or images that describe it. Gendlin proposes a process of:

1 Clear a space
2 Locate felt sense
3 Find a handle – descriptive words or images
4 Resonate word or image with felt sense
5 Receive the shift that occurs due to this realisation

The process is open ended and Gendlin stated it is a universal human activity. Others have developed the process slightly to fit their needs. Foxcroft (2005) talks about listening to one's self with compassion and offers the following phases:

1 Deciding – turning to the source
2 Resonating – the place has a unique feel, quality, mood or tone
3 Sensing-and-welcoming – returning to the body to look for a fit with a word, image, sound or gesture

The paths to supporting others to achieve this for Foxcroft (2005) are:

1 Befriending – we sit down quietly next to the feeling
2 Actively un-knowing – we can't know what may come
3 Listening to one another with compassion

Foxcroft's model has been formulated as:

1 deciding
2 inviting
3 befriending
4 wondering
5 returning

(Jordan 2016)

Focusing leads to greater awareness described as '*presence*' which can facilitate the development of a compassionate, accepting relationship. Bio-spiritual focusing, developed by Roman Catholic priests Peter Campbell and Edwin McMahon, similarly describes a caring, feeling presence and its ability to welcome whatever a person is with kindness and acceptance.

Summary of self

Self – *it is the interaction between an individual's 'felt sense' which provides meaning through embodied relational knowing and the world in which the person lives in time and space.*

This definition identifies that there is more to the self than a collection of enduring traits or the role a person undertakes. This fits well with the gestalt saying 'the whole is greater than the sum of its parts'. The cognitive behavioural definition of the person offers a measurement of some of the parts, which has its uses, but this phenomenological psychological perspective offers a view of the self that is something more than the sum of the parts. The focus of this book is on mental wellbeing and almost all methods of developing and maintaining mental wellbeing involve knowledge of self.

Resilience

Within an individualist society and an existential philosophical tradition there is the expectation that people are responsible for themselves and have the power to maintain and manage their personal wellbeing. Within Western cultures there has been a focus on how individuals can manage their own health and wellbeing which has led to the development of focus on resilience. Ann Masten (2001) indicated that resilience developed as a result of the work conducted to evaluate the adversity of severe life events on children and families such as wars.

The etymology of the word 'resilience' is from the Latin verb '*resilire*' meaning to 'leap back' or 'spring back'. When used in psychology, this term usually describes the ability to recover from negative emotional experiences and flexibly adapt to the requirements of stressful experiences (Hu *et al.* 2014). Resilience is the ability to be flexible and adaptable in response to internal or external stressors in a way that maintains personal wellbeing (Barker 2016). The concept of resilience is still, though, contested with differing operational definitions (Herrman *et al.* 2011). The main issue with definitions, similar to the articulating self, is whether resilience is a trait or a dynamic process which has been circumvented in the definition given here.

Resilience has been identified as a category of personality traits and as a process, which indicates that its definition lies within the cognitive behavioural perspective. It has been associated with individuals' exposure to stressful and adverse events and their ability to adjust or adapt. The personality traits that are linked to maintaining wellbeing at times of stress are:

- Positive attitude/Easy temperament
- Optimism and sense of humour/Good self-esteem
- Active coping/Good planning skills
- Cognitive flexibility/Mental flexibility
- Moral compass

(Barker 2016)

Michael Rutter (1987) explained that resilience is recognised by six significant predictors that include:

- Stressors: factors that trigger the resilience process and disrupt the state of homeostasis in the individual, family or society
- External environmental context: the balance of risk and protective factors
- Person-environment interactional processes: the interaction between the individual and environment. It recognises the individual's efforts to understand and overcome stressful environments
- Internal self-characteristics: physical, emotional, cognitive, behavioural and spiritual strengths to develop protective situations or adaptive experiences
- Resilience processes: short- and long-term resilience processes learnt by exposure to stressful challenges or experiences
- Positive outcomes: successful adaptation to life, stressful situations and traumatic experiences

Robertson and Cooper (2013) identified four key components of resilience:

- Adaptability
- Confidence
- Social support
- Purposefulness

The core personality type or collection of traits has been labelled '*ego resilience*'. People exhibiting this are said to be optimistic, curious and have the mental capacity to conceptualise problems (Barker 2016). Along with these individual traits some researchers have focused on the social aspects of resilience, identifying good support networks such as family members (Herrman *et al.* 2011). Resilience has also been conceptualised as a process. Culture, lifespan stage, and adaptive strategies influence responses to adverse experiences with resilience as the motivating force leading to social and psychological outcomes (Davydov *et al.* 2010).

Resilience defined using a cognitive behavioural perspective, as a construct of personality or a conceptual process, is useful in a contemporary exploration of the phenomenon. Health psychologists recognising the importance of resilience have applied it to their underlying principle of a bio-psychosocial model of the person in recognition that resilience is not only a group of personality traits or a process; it is a complex phenomenon.

Complex phenomena can be reduced to cognitive behavioural definitions such as the traits and processes approach which provide researchers with the opportunity to undertake traditional scientific studies but as with self and wellbeing this is at risk of losing the richness of the phenomenon. Given the temporal and embodied features of resilience, any phenomenological study is likely to have quite disparate findings depending on the participant group. For example, Liersch-Sumskis (2013) found striving to be a key component for people with schizophrenia whereas Hassani *et al.* (2017) found fortitude, lifespan adjustment, disease processes and spirituality to be key factors in a group of elderly people with chronic diseases. Despite the essence of the phenomenon appearing to be very different for each of these studies, they both relate to Morse's (2000) phenomenological research into suffering. Morse (2000) found two types of suffering: enduring and emotional release. From the two studies identified here the older people appear to be using an enduring approach and the people with schizophrenia appear to be emotionally dynamic.

Resilience using a phenomenological perspective could, though, be defined in a similar manner to self; *it is deriving meaning from the interaction between an individual's 'felt sense' through embodied relational knowing of self, others and the world in which they live in time and space to facilitate a sense of wellbeing.*

Bio-psychosocial model of resilience

A bio-psychosocial model of resilience incorporates the major elements included in other psychological health models, in this case harm reduction, protective factors and promotion factors at the level of intrapersonal, interpersonal and society. This bio-psychosocial model which underpins health psychology can offer a structure for understanding and exploring resilience; see Table 3.1.

Resilience, whether regarded as personality traits, a process or a bio-psychosocial matrix, has been found to actively enhance positive psychological wellbeing (Davydov *et al.* 2010). Therefore, we need to consider how it can be developed and enhanced.

Resilience is about maintaining wellbeing in adversity; its origin lies in both experience and underlying psychological make-up, but it is not a fixed trait, and can be developed (Robertson and Cooper 2013). There is some evidence to suggest it can be developed through cognitive behavioural therapy (CBT) training workshops which teach cognitive appraisal and stress

Table 3.1 Bio-psychosocial matrix for understanding resilience

	Harm reduction	*Protective factors*	*Promotion*
Intrapersonal	What elements within the person reduce risk of harm? For example, personality traits	What elements within the person provide protection? For example, emotional coping strategies	What elements within the person facilitate promotion of their wellbeing? For example, problem solving coping strategies
Interpersonal	What elements between people reduce risk of harm? For example, emotional support	What elements between people provide protection? For example, social support	What elements between people facilitate promotion of their wellbeing? For example, role modelling
Society	What elements within organisations reduce risk of harm? For example, policies and legislation	What elements within organisations provide protection? For example, structures which facilitate social support	What elements within organisations facilitate promotion of their wellbeing? For example, personal development reviews

management techniques such as defusing catastrophic thinking, dealing with counterproductive beliefs, cognitive problem solving, developing social support networks and enhanced coping strategies (Stewart and Terry 2014). Social networks are a significant factor in resilience and the family resilience theory recognises the complex role of family interaction and its influence in developing or limiting individuals' strengths. Family resilience is a significant factor that encompasses family support, communication, shared beliefs and structure.

CBT proposes that dysfunctional underlying assumptions are the foundation for mental distress in times of adversity and Seligman's 3P's Model of Resilience indicates that there are three distortions that can challenge an individual's ability to recover from adverse life events, which are:

- Personalisation: a cognitive distortion that makes the individual blame themselves for every problem and recognise themselves as the failure.
- Pervasiveness: an individual perceives that every event affects each part of their life, not just one part, which reduces their successful comprehension of and adaptability to the event.
- Permanence: outlines individuals' perception that an adverse event or its effects will continue to persist forever.

There are problems with using resilience as a therapeutic approach to develop or maintain wellbeing as it could indicate that wellbeing is under the control of the individual. Wellbeing is a subjective experience and whilst a cognitive behavioural approach such as one outlined in the development of resilience is a useful tool for those seeking to improve a person's wellbeing, it can never be complete without acknowledgement of '*felt sense*', more than the sum of the parts.

Resilience has been identified as a requirement for working in areas that require high emotional labour to reduce burnout, but Gilbert's theory of a compassion-focused model and therapy highlights the need for self-compassion. When a person has self-compassion, they show themselves to be understanding (self-empathy), sensitive, to have distress tolerance and a non-judgemental regard for themselves. The need to provide compassionate care could be enhancing for wellbeing, not draining, using this approach (Barker and Williams 2018). This was seen earlier in the chapter when exploring Rogers' and Gendlin's theories of the being and becoming a person. It is also important to remember that although individuals' responses to stress may vary, many of the body systems are correlated with resilience (Southwick 2012).

Self-compassion

Paul Gilbert is a clinical psychologist who developed an underpinning theory and process of applying a model of compassion to psychotherapy. Compassion-focused therapy (Gilbert 2009) is an integrated approach that draws upon evolutionary, social, developmental and Buddhist psychology and neuroscience. Gilbert observed that people with high levels of shame and self-criticism, often rooted in early trauma or abuse, experience difficulties in being kind to themselves or being self-compassionate. He hypothesised that in these individuals, the affect systems (regulating emotions) that help people to feel content and register human warmth are out of balance. Rebalancing the systems is seen as one goal of compassion-focused therapy with an emphasis on developing the social safeness/soothing system.

The therapy involves CBT type training, but the skills are offered in an overall environment of warmth, kindness and support, which can be likened to Rogers' therapeutic relationship. The focus of this therapy is to teach the person to generate an emotion towards themselves of self-warmth or self-kindness, or, as Gilbert defines it, self-compassion.

Chapter summary

This chapter initially explored some of the most well-known social theories of self: self-concept, personality. All of them have their foundations in the behavioural perspective. Therefore, they all involve some level of learning with the later and more cognitive theories all including classical, operant and social learning. These cognitive theories (SIT, dramaturgical, looking glass self, social comparison) also involve observation of self and others leading to self-evaluation and management. These support a cognitive psychological definition of *personality, the relatively stable traits or characteristics demonstrated by a person over time*. They also lead to more individualistic methods to gain a sense of wellbeing such as 'resilience' and 'self-compassion'.

The second part of the chapter went on to explore what was meant by subjective self, proposing an alternative definition of self. Self is *the interaction between an individual's 'felt sense' which provides meaning through embodied relational knowing and the world in which the person lives in time and space*. This definition identifies that there is more to the self than a collection of enduring traits or the role a person undertakes. This fits well with the famous gestalt saying '*the whole is greater than the sum of its parts*'. The cognitive behavioural definition of the person offers an opportunity for measurement of some of the parts, which has its uses, but this phenomenological psychological perspective offers a view of the self that is something more than the sum of the parts. The focus of this book is on mental wellbeing and almost all methods of developing and maintaining mental wellbeing involve knowledge of self.

The third and last part of this chapter explored resilience and self-compassion, both of which are individualistic therapies that help a person to develop self-understanding and wellbeing. Research has demonstrated that they have been beneficial in the improvement of a sense of wellbeing. A more profound self-understanding may be achieved, though, through focusing and engaging with one's felt sense which, if associated with unconditional positive regard, could lead to a profound sense of self and mental wellbeing.

References

Barker, S. 2016. *Psychology for Nurses and Health Care Practitioners to Support Compassionate Care*. London: Sage, p. 159.

Barker, S. 2018. "Embodied Recovery Environments". *In*: Norman, I. and Ryrie, I. (Eds.) *The Art and Science of Mental Health Nursing*. London: OUP, Chapter 10.

Barker, S., Williams, S. 2018. "Compassionate Communication" *In*: Wright, K. and McKeown, M. (Eds.) *Essentials of Mental Health Nursing*. London: Sage, Chapter 20.

Campbell, P., McMahon, E. 1997. *Bio-Spirituality – Focusing as a Way to Grow*. Chicago, Illinois: Loyola Press.

Chatard, A., Bocage-Barthelemy, Y., Selimbeggovic, L., Guimond, S. 2017. "The Woman Who Wasn't There: Converging Evidence That Subliminal Comparison Affects Self-evaluation", *Journal of Experimental Social Psychology*, 73, November, 1–13.

Davydov, D.M., Stewart, R., Ritchie, K., Chaudieu, I. 2010. "Resilience and Mental Health", *Clinical Psychology Review*, 30, 479–495.

Foxcroft, R. 2005. Touching the Source. Available at: www.focusing.org.uk/touching-the-source.

Gilbert, P. 2009. "Introducing Compassion-focused Therapy", *Advances in Ppsychiatric Treatment*, 15, 199–208.

Goffman, E. 1959. *The Presentation of Self in Everyday Life*. New York: Doubleday.
Guimond, S. 2006. *Social Comparison and Social Psychology: Understanding Cognition, Intergroup Relations, and Culture*. New York: Cambridge University Press.
Hassani, P., Izadi-Avanji, F.S., Rakshan, M., Alavi Maind, H. 2017. "A Phenomenological Study on Resilience of the Elderly Suffering from Chronic Disease: A Qualitative Study", *Psychology Research and Behavior Management,* 10, 59–67.
Heidegger, M. 2008. *Being and Time*. New York: HarperPerennial.
Herrman, H., Stewart, D.E., Diaz-Granados, N., Berger, E.L., Jackson, B., Yuen, T. 2011. "What Is Resilience?" *The Canadian Journal of Psychiatry*, 2011, 56, 5, 258–265.
Hochschild, A. 1983. *The Managed Heart: Commercialization of Human Feeling*. Berkeley: University of California Press.
Hu, T., Zhang, D., Wang, J. 2015. "A Meta-analysis of the Trait Resilience and Mental Health", *Personality and Individual Differences*, 76, 18–27.
Johnson, K. 2015. "Behavioral Education in the 21st Century", *Journal of Organizational Behavior Management*, 35, 1–2, 135–150. DOI: 0.1080/01608061.2015.1036152.
Jordan, S. 2016. An Introduction to Focusing. Available at: www.focusing.org.uk/an-introduction-to-focusing.
Liersch-Sumskis, S. 2013. A Phenomenological Examination of the Meaning of Resilience as Described by People Who Experience Schizophrenia. Ph.D thesis. University of Wollongong.
Luft, J., Ingham, H. 1955. "Johari Window, a Graphic Model of Interpersonal Awareness". *In*: Luft J. 1969. *Of Human Interaction*. Palo Alto, CA: National Press.
Masten, A.S. 2001. "Ordinary Magic: Resilience Processes in Development", *American Psychologist*, 56, 3, 227–238.
McCoy, C.A. 2017. "Playing Goffman's Information Game: A Classroom Activity Involving Student Interactions", *Teaching Sociology*, 45, 3, 260–268.
Morse, J.M. 2000. "Responding to the Cues of Suffering", *Health Care for Women International*, 21, 1–9.
Mussweiler, T. 2003. "Comparison Processes in Social Judgment. Mechanisms and Consequences", *Psychological Review*, 110 (2003), 472–489. DOI: 10.1037/0033-295X.110.3.472.
O'Mahen, H.A., Moberly, N.J., Wright, K.A. 2019. "Trajectories of Change in a Group Behavioral Activation Treatment for Severe, Recurrent Depression", *Behavior Therapy*, 50 (2019), 504–514.
Reich, S., Schneider, F.M., Heling, L. 2018. "Zero Likes – Symbolic Interactions and Need Satisfaction Online", *Computers in Human Behavior*, 80 (2018), 97–102.
Robertson, I., Cooper, C.L. 2013. "Resilience", *Stress and Health*, 29, 175–176.
Rogers, C.R. 1951. *Client Centred Therapy*. London: Constable.
Rogers, C.R. 1957. "The Necessary and Sufficient Conditions of Therapeutic Personality Change", *Journal of Consulting Psychology*, 21, 2, 95–103.
Siljanovska, L., Stojcevska, S. 2018. "A Critical Analysis of Interpersonal Communication in Modern Times of the Concept 'Looking Glass Self (1902)' by Charles Horton Cooley", *SEEU Review*, 13, 1, 62–74. DOI: https://doi.org/10.2478/seeur-2018-0007.
Skinner, B.F. 1965. *Science and Human Behavior*. New York: The Free Press.
Southwick, S.M., Charney, D.S. 2012. *Resilience: The Science of Mastering Life's Greatest Challenges*. Cambridge: Cambridge University Press.

Stewart, W., Terry, L. 2014. "Reducing Burnout in Nurses and Care Workers in Secure Settings", Nursing Standard, 28, 34, 37–45.

Suls, J., Martin, R., Wheeler, L. 2002. "Social Comparison: Why, With Whom, and With What Effect?", *Current Directions in Psychological Science*, 11 (2002), 159–163.

Todres, L. 2007. *Embodied Enquiry: Phenomenological Touchstones for Research, Psychotherapy and Spirituality*. Basingstoke: Palgrave Macmillan.

Waldbuesser, C. 2019. "Who Are You? Teaching Symbolic Interaction and Perceptions of the Self in the Classroom", *Communication Teacher*, 33, 2, 99–102. DOI: 10.1080/17404622.2018.1536798.

Watson, J.B., Raynor R. 1920. "Conditioned Emotional Reaction", *Journal of Experimental Psychology*, 3, 1, February 1920, 1–14. Available at: www.scribd.com/document/250748771/Watson-and-Raynor-1920.

Chapter 4

History, temporality and culture

Introduction

In contemporary society there is a passion for exploring the past from palaeontology and archaeology to genealogy, more recent family members and biographies of the not yet dead. This is clearly demonstrated in television listings, social media and newspapers (see Box 4.1). This information, particularly anything that links and situates the individual within a family or network, can lead to emotional reactions and therefore one's sense of wellbeing. This sense of wellbeing is fundamentally linked to the person's sense of identity within time and place.

Box 4.1 Examples of media focused on history

There are numerous examples of television programmes and websites available to get in touch with one's 'roots', in fact one such film was called *Roots* and led the viewers through a traumatic presentation of the experiences of Africans taken as slaves to America.

Some examples of such television documentary programmes and films are:

Meet the Ancestors
Time Team
Blowing Up History
Little Sparta
Back in Time for Brixton
What the Industrial Revolution Did for Us
The Unwanted: The Secret Windrush Files

Some examples of websites are:

Ancestry.co.uk
Findmypast.co.uk
Familytreedna.com
Familysearch.org

All the theories considered in the exploration of self in Chapter 3 adhere to the psychological philosophy of personal continuity except, perhaps, Goffman's dramaturgical theory of the self. They indicate that there is something that we identify as ourselves that is different from others and continues over time. In Western societies there is also an acceptance that people have continuing essential needs across time and culture, which are greater than those needed to attribute life. To establish people's needs Maslow's (1943) triangular hierarchy is a useful starting point. For all forms of life, as with Maslow's hierarchy of needs (1943), it is accepted that basic physical and safety needs have priority. For Maslow once these are addressed people require the fulfilment of psychological needs such as esteem and belonging to not only develop wellbeing but also to maintain it.

In keeping with most published definitions of wellbeing, Historic England offer the following: "Wellbeing is quality of life and prosperity, positive physical and mental health, sustainable thriving communities" (Reilly *et al.* 2018) but their relational element is geographical. Subjective self and wellbeing are both conceptualised by individual perceptions, but despite this they are influenced by the dimensions of time and place. Wellbeing in time and place includes the socio-political environment as well as geography. "*Wellbeing is politically and conceptually linked with addressing health inequality and social cohesion*" (ibid) and Reilly *et al.*, on behalf of Historic England, offer a framework of six features identifying the link between heritage and wellbeing (see Table 4.1).

Table 4.1 Framework of wellbeing linked to heritage adapted from Reilly *et al.* (2018)

Feature	*Action*	*Impact*
Process	Volunteering, being useful	Development of self-esteem, meaning and competence
Participation	Cultural engagement	An increase in self-awareness, self-expression, sense of belonging and ability to relate to others by seeing things from different perspectives
Mechanism	Social interaction, reminiscence, sharing	Developing creativity and connection, sense of belonging
Healing	Assessment of patients, handling museum objects	Facilitates thinking and meaning-making, self-esteem and positive interactions
Place	'Place-shaping' – ensuring that local people have a voice	Developing belonging, connection, pride, meaning, cultural identity, sense of empowerment and belonging
Environment	Interacting with nature and historical artefacts	Developing wellbeing

As part of their framework heritage is defined as awareness and engagement with history personally (ancestry, genealogy, identity, values, ownership) or publicly (culture, customs, traditions, values, national treasures).

People live and experience the world from a unique position in time and place. History, ancestry and genealogy can only occur once temporal and spatial dimensions are acknowledged. Discrete historical events, as well as the historical evolution of cultural norms and values, economic organisation and technologies, help shape places and people. The events that unfold throughout history change places and people by changing the composition of populations inducing movement, and the situations of individuals who remain.

Understanding of ancestry situated in a changing politico-social history is considered essential to understanding one's self and their basic humanity and diversity: "It informs our sense of identity and place in contemporary culture, geographical and historical space" (Nicholson 2018: 29). To know who we really are, our heritage, and where we came from, where our past became our present and how the past may be influencing the present, is a human need. This need can be summed up in three fundamental questions:

- The past – Where do I come from?
- The present – Why am I here?
- The future – What is going to happen to me?

This has been labelled by Thomas Fuchs (2013) as explicit subjective temporality (time), and he also described an implicit subjective temporality which will be explored later in the chapter. Explicit subjective temporality, conscious awareness of time, is experienced as closely bound up with certain time-specific emotions.

- The present: the 'now' with surprise, astonishment or shock
- The past: the 'no longer' with regret, grief or remorse
- The future: the 'not yet' with desire, impatience, yearning or hope

People living in contemporary society can access many avenues through which to explore their history. With new technologies individuals can determine their ancestry through methods such as genetic testing. This not only gives them information about their most likely origins, but it can also determine what is likely to influence their future biologically and politically. It can provide an historical ethnic identity (such as who counts as Cherokee or Maori), religious identity (who counts as Parsee or Jewish), family identity (who counts as a descendant of Winston Churchill), or caste (who counts as Brahman or Dalit) (Elliott and Brodwin 2002), all of which will influence interactions with others and access to opportunities, therefore having an impact on who the person is and their likely sense of wellbeing.

Whilst genetics, biology, offers one prism through which to explore historical identity and wellbeing, these biological indicators only offer a narrow and frequently contested viewpoint. Anthropologists such as Friedman (1992) present a constructivist understanding of identity and ancestry which builds upon both biological and social foundations. He asserts that the past is "always practised in the present" because people mould their understanding and knowledge of the past in present actions (1992: 854). Friedman states "The constitution of identity is an elaborate and deadly serious game of mirrors. It is a complex temporal interaction of multiple practices of identification external and internal to a subject or population" (ibid). The motivation to construct an historical identity in this way is to give meaning to where we have come from.

It is an act of self-identification which needs to be an authentic interpretation of the relationship between the existence of the individual and a world that makes sense. This relationship may exist in a myriad of ways due to the number of different social orders and practices in historically, spatially and socially determined circumstances (Friedman 1992).

Experiences of temporality

Whilst Friedman (1992) established the importance of historical (or temporal), spatial and social determinants of self-identification through his anthropological studies, Fuchs (2013) also recognises the importance of these from a phenomenological philosophical perspective. He identifies three features of temporality: implicit subjective temporality, explicit subjective temporality and intersubjective temporality.

Implicit subjective temporality is where the person is unconsciously moving towards their personal goals, they are becoming themselves, in a way that feels timeless. Explicit subjective temporality occurs when the person is 'awoken' or made conscious of time through some external stimuli; they have conscious awareness of past, present and future with all the emotions this may invoke as identified above. Intersubjective temporality suggests a shared understanding of time and place; it is relational. People experience a resonance at a biological level through a continuous adaptation of endogenous and exogenous rhythms such as days, months, years.

This synchronicity of people is influenced by feedback from their social environment. This is achieved through daily contact with others and becoming attuned through bodily, emotional and interactional communication. This is demonstrated in the early development of attachment between a small child and their primary caregiver. The child and caregiver attune to one another; they develop attunement through a melodic rhythm of facial expressions, gestures and vocalisations (see Box 4.2). Whilst synchronicity is the aim of these early relationships, for some intersubjective temporality may be dyssynchronous. Dyssynchronous intersubjective temporality tends to occur during times of explicit temporality (conscious awareness of time).

Box 4.2 Mother–child interaction

I watch my daughter-in-law and my grandson as they gaze into each other's eyes. She speaks to him gently, each absorbed in the reality of the other, outside of time and space. I sit here in their living room conscious of having no part in the interaction. I feel alone and isolated; it is only momentary but feels like a lifetime. Then I move and break the moment, and feel guilty as if I have broken a magical spell. My grandson turns his face to me and smiles which suddenly takes me back to a time when his father was his age: the smile, the look, the same. It generates an explosion in my chest, tingling, which radiates around my body. I'm suddenly in a different time and place, I'm gazing into my son's eyes and he into mine and we are having a conversation; I tell him he is wonderful, and he gurgles and touches my face, I kiss his hand and he giggles. We are the centre of the universe; no one else exists despite being here in this room with others. I feel loved, special, transcended to something more than I can describe. Suddenly I'm brought back to the room and smile at my grandson, a poignant, calm, attentive and engaged smile.

Soulful space

Fuchs' understanding of temporality and wellbeing has foundations in the philosophical approach of Heidegger. Heidegger, in his book *Being and Time*, identifies spatiality, temporality, intersubjectivity and embodiment as part of human experience, their ontology. Initially Gendlin developed Heidegger's philosophical writing to explore how this could be helpful to people not experiencing wellbeing. Todres took this further and developed what he called '*soulful space*' as part of his philosophical psychotherapeutic practice (2007), leading individuals from a position of dyssynchronicity and illbeing to synchronicity and wellbeing.

Todres (2004) uses the word 'soulful' not in a religious faith sense but more in a Western cultural sense of evoking deep feeling or emotion. It is the ability to access a 'soulful space', a moment in time and space where the person can accept themselves, in their entirety, including their vulnerability, to have a deep sense of who they are and who they are becoming. Accepting a 'soulful space' indicates a kind of freedom, a freedom to embrace the whole of oneself, to acknowledge one's full humanity. Soulful space correlates with Gendlin's (1987) description of a kind of 'flow' of 'being-with' where human vulnerability, need and 'unfinishedness' of oneself is embraced. This is a natural moving from past through the present accepting the future will bring change. Not only do people need to understand themselves and their personal history but also how this fits with their sense of others and others' history.

Todres states that,

> A compassion for vulnerability may be an important existential task in a world that still easily lurches towards fantasies, systems and technologies

> of hoped-for invulnerability and purity, with its vision of a great transcendent winner; a vision of power rather than inclusive empathy.
>
> (2004: 1)

Inclusive empathy supports and is supported by a synchronous intersubjective temporality. Philosophically the conception of temporal and spatial subjective and intersubjective experiences provide a platform for self-understanding and wellbeing. When these concepts are not acknowledged dyssynchronous intersubjective experiences could occur, leading to reduced empathy and wellbeing. Todres (2004) states that soulfulness recognises and accepts individual heartfelt historical moments. It includes the things that we are touched by, being open to others and temporality. At this point some may question the difference between 'soulful space' and 'mindfulness'. Briefly it is philosophical depth; mindfulness is about being in the moment and aware of it (see Box 4.3) and whilst gaining a soulful space also requires this it is something more. It is a deeper self-recognition and acceptance of the self, situated in time and facing mortality.

Box 4.3 Mindfulness

"Mindfulness is awareness that arises through paying attention, on purpose, in the present moment, non-judgementally," says Kabat-Zinn (2019). It is an abstract concept which needs to be experienced but involves:

- Quiet mental space
- Experiencing the present
- Being in the 'here and now'
- True presence
- Stillness
- Contentment
- Being aware
- Paying attention
- Focusing on the present

Minds are rarely still and these continuous thoughts and feelings can drain energy and get in the way of experiencing pleasure and contentment of the present. There are usually seven attitudes within mindfulness training: beginner's mind, non-striving, letting go, acceptance, non-judging, patience and trust.

Beginner's mind – this is the start to becoming aware of the assumptions and beliefs which get in the way of seeing things as they are. It is the willingness and attention to what is happening rather than relying on previous experience.

Non-striving – in everyday life the tasks engaged with are associated with a certain outcome or change occurring. Stopping striving allows time to reduce the burden of responsibility and guilt, opening the possibility of different outcomes; make space for miracles.

Letting go – There are certain thoughts, beliefs or feelings that are held onto that are unhelpful. Wanting things to be a certain way or wanting other people to act in particular way can be a cause of tension and stress.

Acceptance – When difficult things happen in life there is a tendency to deny or argue about the situation which can prolong the discomfort. Accepting the situation can open up problem solving and moving forward.

Non-judging – there is a constant stream of judgements about situations and other people ongoing in individuals' minds. Standing back and not judging allows fresh assessments and responses to the situation/person rather than reacting based on habits and prejudices.

Patience – people need to be patient and gentle with themselves and others. Patience gives the room to allow what is there to be there and not be in a hurry to change it or ourselves.

Trust – becoming more present and aware through mindfulness, people become more able to listen to their feelings. This helps them to identify the most useful responses to situations and start to trust themselves more.

Phenomenological archaeology

Todres' soulful space can be recognised in what has been labelled as phenomenological archaeology. The archaeologist takes time to enter the space and time of an artefact or geographical place to gain an understanding of the lived experience of the people who resided there or used the artefact at a particular time. Christopher Tilley's *A Phenomenology of Landscape* (1994) was perhaps the first publication to explore this phenomenon. He identified that exploring archaeology without using the whole sensory experience did not allow the rich tapestry of ancient worlds to be realised. It could also reduce understanding of self and others and synchronicity that could be gained in this activity.

It is important here to distinguish between space and place; Harrison and Dournish (1996: 67) define place as "a combination of space and meaning". This was further developed by Gustafson (2001) who identified three areas of meanings related to places:

- Self – including emotions and self-identity
- Environment – including the physical features of the place
- Events – the experiences and relational elements (behaviours and characteristics of those sharing the place)

Malpas (2018) states that the past, a sense of place and human experience are fundamentally linked and an understanding of each cannot be grasped independently, which offers at least in part some explanation for contemporary society's fascination with history. His phenomenological approach to archaeology does not rely solely upon uncovering, measuring and documenting objects, structures and landscapes. As with Tilley (1994) he identified that to understand ancient history there is a need to engage with its qualitative aspects.

Malpas and Tilley use their bodily experiences to engage with places as they move around landscapes which assists with investigation into the social and cultural meaning that might be associated with it. Tilley highlights that whilst traditional archaeologists focus on and describe the physical world it is still experienced by the person on a sensory and emotional level. The place and its history are intertwined with humans. It is a two-way relationship; people influence the place and the place influences the person within time.

Ma

To engage with history to enhance a sense of mental wellbeing, the Stiwdio Arts Group was led to explore Rookwood, a closing down hospital with an eventful history (see Box 4.4). The group were not guided to use phenomenology, but they did receive an explanation on Japanese *ma* and what it was. People struggling with their wellbeing frequently feel cluttered and have difficulty adjusting their focus. *Ma* is the 'space between'; it can be the breath between words, where the sun shines through the leaves, the place on the wall without a picture. It is a negative space balancing the cluttered mind. The group could be considered to have used phenomenological reduction or to have accessed *ma*.

Box 4.4 'Through the Trees' description

At the beginning of the project we were introduced to the large archive associated with Rookwood Hospital that moved from the building's foundations and family home through its role as Red Cross Hospital during the war to the present hospital that is being closed as it is no longer fit for purpose. We spent some time reflecting on the phases of the building, imagining the house and garden parties, the development of the arboretum, the ladies' involvement with politics and emancipation, the soldiers sent there to recover from their injuries to the present occupants who have experienced some kind of head injury.

One member of the group told us how her grandfather had been admitted there during the Second World War and she had brought along photos to share with us. The conservationists demonstrated how they restored and preserved the paper archives and we were given the opportunity to individually explore them.

In the second workshop we were shown around the hospital grounds following the arboreal trail. We were encouraged to take our time to not only see

> the individual but also parts of the trees. We experienced the majestic Wellingtonias with a sense of awe; the two Wellingtonias standing on the main lawn mark the birth of Sir Edward and Lady Hill's sons. We moved on along the trail to the eerie, foreboding and dark ancient yews with their feeling of timelessness and evergreen needles. Many of the trees were just springing into life and the weak sunshine was being broken up by the twigs, shoots and small uncurling leaves, offering hope of a bright future. From the hopefulness we entered the open space where a solitary mulberry tree with angular, brittle leaflessness stood out despite the ivy trying to consume it. The path then took us round to the front of the neogothic building with the spring sunshine highlighting the beautiful magnolia tree with its large tulip shaped flowers. As we came upon this tree I could feel the atmosphere lighten and the group smiled.

Studies have explored the relationship of history-related activities with wellbeing. They have found that history-related activities such as participation in museum and heritage sites can provide people with a sense of belonging, access to memories and emotions (Ashton and Kean 2012; Kean and Martin 2013; Lloyd and Moore 2015). They can also enable the construction of identity and stories for people, their families and communities (Smith 2006). Oral historians, through reminiscence (Bonnett and Alexander 2013) and sociologists alike, have promoted the positive impact on wellbeing through identity work and the impact of connection on emotion (Kramer 2011).

Defence Archaeology Group

The studies showing a link between wellbeing and archaeology along with the needs of veterans have led to the development of organisations such as the Defence Archaeology Group (DAG). This was set up in order to facilitate recovery from physical and mental health problems for veterans who had undergone traumatic experiences (Finnegan 2016). The benefits gained from these activities were improved self-esteem, confidence, a reduction in stigma and motivation to seek help. It was also found that improved mood was associated with the experience. The researchers concluded this was due to being in a supportive familiar environment where skills already held could be exercised and new friends could be made.

It would appear the studies associated with this organisation show that, despite improving their sense of wellbeing through engagement and being interested in history, it was the cultural aspects that had the biggest impact. As indicated by Smith (2006), it is not the objects and places that are intrinsically valuable, it is the way in which they can become a vehicle to assert and affirm the values that underpin different communities. The stories that cultures support and develop over time are what allow people to give meaning to themselves and their sense of place.

Culture

> Culture is socially determined and shapes many aspects of our identity, including our beliefs, values and behaviour. It encompasses many factors, including race, ethnicity, religion, gender, sexuality, age, generation, class, life experience and lifestyle.
>
> (Thurgood 2009: 630)

Culture has been described as the 'lens' through which the world can be seen. It includes a set of assumptions about the world which may be expressed symbolically through language, art and ritual; culture is our worldview (Draper and McSheery 2007).

Further to the socially determined definition of Thurgood, Napoles *et al.* (2010: 390) offer a consensual definition of culture; he writes, "A consensual definition of culture found in the literature is that it consists of shared group behaviours and norms, such as traditions, values, beliefs, attitudes, symbols, language, religion and social roles of an ethnic group". This can be interpreted as culture being the shared meanings a distinct group of people use to colour and manage their everyday experiences.

Kitwood (1997) offers a similar definition; he states that culture is the patterns of behaviour that give meaning to experiences and provide structure for group actions and interactions. For these theorists culture is the outward expression of shared meaning which occurs at a particular time and place.

Culture can be experienced consciously or unconsciously; people are able to be consciously aware of their culture, and that of others, as with time and place, but it can also influence behaviour at an unconscious level. It has been suggested that there are three main elements of culture: its knowledge or power base, behavioural norms and an ideology or belief system. Kitwood (1997) identified through his research into dementia care cultures that dominant cultures or hegemonies are difficult to change.

Ideologies underpinning culture

Rothman (2000) also indicated that cultures are underpinned by ideologies. These ideologies or worldviews, or to use the 'lens' analogy the direction in which the person faces, influence their sense of themselves and their interactions. There are three powerful political ideologies in most cultures: patriarchy, technology and the socialism capitalism construct. These ideologies can be explained as follows:

Patriarchy is a system that values masculine thought processes and behaviours above feminine ones, although in contemporary Western society the distinction between genders has become more blurred. It has been suggested this has led to a valuing of biomedical approaches to health where the professional knows best and the patient humbly accepts their intervention or lack of it.

Technology is a value system that privileges what is new and innovative over what is old and familiar. Technology or technocracy, as it has been labelled, focuses on the 'how' of living, not the 'why'. It can destroy tradition because it refuses any limits on its freedom to be creative. It is strongly linked to the politics of economics where the ability to function economically is important and valued. Within this ideology technology provides the mechanism for health and wellbeing regardless of ethics. It leads to the belief that if the technology has been created it should be available.

Capitalism/socialism – these are suggested opposing ends of a spectrum of political-economic ideologies where capitalism puts a higher value on individual freedom and socialism or communism a higher value on justice. Both ethical principles (freedom/justice) are valued regardless of societal ideology, but which one forms the basis of the hegemony is particularly important when used as a political construct. Capitalism could lead to health and wellbeing becoming commodities which can be bought and sold which some will not be able to afford, whereas socialism might lead to health and wellbeing being accepted as a universal human need which should be freely available to everyone.

The early twenty-first century, in the UK, has seen a move towards non-intervention by government with a movement away from paternalism towards self-reliance (Forbat 2008) and, it could be suggested, a more capitalist society. This promotes self-efficacy and autonomy but if autonomy is the path to achieving wellbeing then for those who lack the ability to self-monitor and be assertive wellbeing will be compromised.

Wellbeing, in this individual political sense, may be problematic for some to achieve but it becomes even more difficult to attain when the social determinants of health and wellbeing are considered. People in individualistic societies, for the most part Western societies, tend to report higher levels of happiness than people in collectivistic ones (socialist/communist) which are not accounted for by socioeconomic factors alone (Suh and Koo 2008). This may relate to collectivistic cultures emphasising the maintenance of social order and harmony leading to the expectation that members suppress their personal desires to promote collective interests. They value self-regulation over the self-expression and self-sufficiency which are highly prized in individualistic cultures.

Globalisation

The cultural hegemony, which is the generally accepted dominant ideology, in Western societies has more recently been identified as globalisation by Hassa Hanafi (2009). He states that disharmony is at risk as the

> threat is actually greater because only one path, one opinion and one ideal is being followed. And anyone who dares to defy, for example,

> Afghanistan, Iraq, Syria, Lebanon, Egypt, Sudan, Saudi Arabia or Yemen must expect military aggression, either through the United Nations, or outside the United Nations. Globalisation is one of the forms of Western hegemony based on the laws of the market and military power.
>
> (Hanafi 2009)

Globalisation has multiple and contested meanings; generically it is described as "the ways in which nations, businesses and people are becoming more connected and interdependent across national borders through increased economic integration, communication, cultural diffusion and travel" (Labonte and Schrecker 2006: 3). Globalisation is one of the key concepts proposed by the World Health Organisation (WHO) of the social determinants of health. Others include employment conditions, social exclusion, public health programmes, women and gender, early child development, health systems and urbanisation (WHO 2019).

For individuals within Western societies there may be a converse assumption made to the one stated by Hanafi above. Within Western contemporary society the globalisation of businesses is believed to blur current definitions of wellbeing. Whilst there is some evidence for this blurring and globalisation as a Western hegemony, anthropologists highlight the need to recognise a multiplicity of 'wellbeings' and suggest the importance of place or context should not be ignored (Mathews and Izquierdo 2009).

The ideologies discussed above underpin most large cultural groups but there are many other smaller micro-cultures, or ways of seeing the world, which can influence wellbeing for those adhering to the cultural hegemony. Professional cultures such as the Nursing Midwifery Council and the General Medical Council have changed over time and the same occurs with other cultures but for some cultures and religious groups there is a focus on orthodoxy and maintaining a strict adherence to certain rules (see Box 4.5).

Box 4.5 Case study – Aastha Patel

Aastha, whose name means faith, arrived in the UK when she was a young woman to marry a man that her parents had chosen for her. She had been living in a rural area of the Indian subcontinent and only had a few words of English when she arrived; her first language was Gujarati. Aastha is a Hindu and as indicated by her name she has been a woman of faith throughout her life. She has been content in her marriage for 40 years and her children have left home. Aastha had taken the opportunities provided in her local community to learn to speak, read and write English, although when her family were at home together, they spoke Gujarati. She encouraged her children and grandchildren to learn and be mindful of their god, to recognise their oneness with nature and the power of chanting. Aastha chooses to wear the traditional sari but her children and husband wear more Western style clothing. Aastha and her husband are vegetarian, as are most Hindus.

Aastha believes she has been a good Hindu but has become increasingly concerned by the behaviour of her children. They do not undertake their duties to care for her; her daughter wears jeans and refuses to wear a headscarf and her sons have moved overseas.

In Box 4.5 the case study of Aastha offers an understanding that those not adhering to the cultural hegemony may experience disharmony, stress and illbeing but it also offers clues as to how those who submit to the cultural hegemony can also experience reduced wellbeing. Aastha's children have adopted the cultural hegemony along with its norms and behaviours but they now find themselves at odds with their cultural heritage, their family microculture. Aastha's religious orthodoxy and her children's acceptance of the cultural hegemony has led to implicit assumptions about their worlds and dyssynchronicity (see Chapter 2).

Spirituality

In the twentieth century there was little recognition given to spirituality in the UK, arguably as a response to the fervent evangelism of the Victorian Christians and the growth in a multicultural society. Spirituality and religious activities have, though, been closely linked to health and wellbeing throughout history with the provision of health care in mediaeval Britain in monasteries and convents. The old psychiatric hospitals, mostly now closed, had their beautiful chapels, and small places of prayer, worship or meditation are still to be found in most UK hospitals today.

Verity and Lee (2011: 16) suggest that the spirit is the 'spark of life' in people. It is this spark of life that demonstrates wellbeing; it is a common saying when someone is unwell is that the 'sparkle' or 'light' has gone out of their eyes. In this situation the spirit of the person is identified as having left the body.

Spirituality is defined by MacKinlay (2001: 152) as "That which lies at the core of each person's being, an essential dimension which brings meaning to life". She identifies, in her model of spirituality adapted for those with dementia, that transcending loss, finding hope and intimacy with god or in relationship with others, are significant features which interact with a sense of meaning for the person. The basis of MacKinlay's model (2011) is that spirituality is mediated through religion, relationships, environment and arts.

Religion is one element of spirituality in MacKinlay's model (2011). A useful definition of religion is that it is a system of faith and worship that usually involves one or more greater being/s: god/s, who have control and

Box 4.6 Case study – Gareth Collier

Gareth was a coal miner for 40 years and retired at 58 on health grounds, as his breathing had become progressively difficult. Gareth now also has a diagnosis of dementia. He is a proud man and very proud of his mining ancestry, and in his youth he was considered the strongest and fittest young man in the local villages. Despite many of his peers attending chapel he could not accept an all-powerful god and considered himself an atheist.

Throughout his life he has fished as a hobby and although he is now escorted when he goes fishing, he appears to gain a sense of meaning for himself and the world by undertaking this activity. Despite failing memory and confusion when his son comes to take him fishing, he is able to find and collect all his fishing gear. They walk to the river without the son prompting him which way to go and Gareth is able to set up his rod, bait his line and flick the rod to get the 'hook, line and sinker' in the best fishing spot. When Gareth sits down with his rod, he can peacefully watch the river with a look of contentment on his face and tell his son fluent stories of previous fishing episodes in minute detail.

deserve worship and obedience; it is theist. Most religions, micro-cultures, have their set rituals and behavioural norms.

Rituals, though, do not have to be religious; they can involve everyday activities such as preparation for bed or eating a meal. Most rituals use symbols; in Catholic Christian orthodoxy the symbols used are the place (church or cathedral), the ornamentation such as religious icons, the music, chanting of liturgy and the types of interactions engaged in. Many activities have ritualistic elements related to wellbeing; the case study of Gareth offers an example of this concept (see Box 4.6).

It can be seen in the case study of Gareth that spirituality with its ritualistic behaviour for him is to do with his ability to find comfort, self-acceptance and a sense of place, where he can be who he is. The sense of being as an embodied and significant person is important to gain a sense of wellbeing.

Summary of chapter

This chapter has taken a journey from identifying the importance of history for self-concept and wellbeing through supporting philosophy including an understanding of time and space onto its place in culture. The evidence base for a link between history and wellbeing is limited by methodological issues but it does indicate that involvement in history supports subjective experiences of wellbeing. Philosophers such as Gendlin, Todres, Tilley and Malpas all identify that there is more to an experience than can be summed up by what can be seen and measured. The rich tapestry of life can only be appreciated by embodied interaction with the world and each other including a recognition that experiences occur in time and space. The chapter finished with a brief exploration of the link between culture and time, recognising that cultures are underpinned by ideologies which change whilst some spiritual beliefs remain consistent.

The culture, which is time, place and ideology bound, lived in can dramatically influence how and if a person experiences a sense of wellbeing.

References

Ashton, P., Kean, H. 2012. *Public History and Heritage Today: People and Their Pasts.* Basingstoke: Palgrave.

Bonnett, A., Alexander, C. 2013. "Mobile Nostalgias: Connecting Visions of the Urban Past, Present and Future Amongst Ex-residents", *Transactions of the Institute of British Geographers*, 38, 391–402.

Draper, P., McSherry, W. 2007. "Culture, Religion and Spirituality". *In*: Nemo, R., Aveyard, B. and Heath, H. (Eds.) *Older People and Mental Health Nursing, A Handbook of Care.* Oxford: Blackwell Publishing, Chapter 9.

Elliott, C., Brodwin, P. 2002. "Identity and Genetic Ancestry Tracing", *BMJ*, December 21, 325, 7378, 1469–1471. DOI: 10.1136/bmj.325.7378.1469.

Finnegan, A. 2016. "The Biopsychosocial Benefits and Shortfalls for Armed Forces Veterans Engaged in Archaeological Activities", *Nurse Education Today*, 47, 15–22.

Forbat, L., Wilkinson, H. 2008. "Where Should People with Dementia Live? Using the Views of Service Users to Inform Models of Care", *British Journal of Learning Disabilities*, 36. DOI: 10.1111/j.1468-3156.2007.00473.x.

Friedman, J. 1992. "The Past in the Future: History and the Politics of Identity", *American Anthropologist*, 94, 4, new series, 837–859. Retrieved from: www.jstor.org/stable/680224.

Fuchs, T. 2013. "Temporality and Psychopathology", *Phenomenology and the Cognitive Sciences*, 12, 75–104. DOI: 10.1007/s11097-010-9189-4.

Gendlin, E.T. 1987. "A Philosophical Critique of the Concept of Narcissism: The Significance of the Awareness Movement". *In*: Levin, D.M. (Ed.) *Pathologies of the Modern Self: Postmodern Studies on Narcissism, Schizophrenia and Depression.* New York: New York University Press, pp. 257–304.

Gustafson, P. 2001. "Meanings of Place: Everyday Experience and Conceptualizations", *Journal of Environmental Psychology*, 21, 1, 5–16.

Hanafi, H. 2009. Globalisation Is Western Hegemony. https://en.qantara.de/content/hassan-hanafi-globalisation-is-western-hegemony.

Harrison, S., Dournish, P. 1996. Re-place-ing Space: The Roles of Place and Space in Collaborative Systems, ACM Conference on Computer Supported Cooperative Work, pp. 67–76.

Heidegger, M. 2008. *Being and Time.* New York: HarperPerennial.

Kabat-Zinn, 2019. Mindful, Healthy Mind, Healthy Life. www.mindful.org/meditation/mindfulness-getting-started/.

Kean, H., Martin, P. 2013. *The Public History Reader.* London: Routledge.

Kitwood, T. 1997. *Dementia Reconsidered: The Person Comes First.* Berkshire: Open University Press.

Kramer, A.M. 2011. "Kinship, Affinity and Connectedness: Exploring the Role of Genealogy in Personal Lives", *Sociology*, 45, 3, 379–395.

Labonte, R., Schrecker, T. 2006. Globalisation and Social Determinants of Health: Analytic and Strategic Review Paper, p. 3. Institute of Population Health. World Health Organisation. www.who.int/social_determinants/themes/globalization/en/.

Lloyd, S., Moore, J. 2015. "Sedimented Histories: Connections, Collaborations and Co-production in Regional History", *History Workshop Journal*, 80, 1, 234–248.

MacKinlay, E. 2011. "Creative Processes to Bring Out Expressions of Spirituality: Working with People Who Have Dementia". *In*: Lee, H., Adams, T. (Eds.) *Creative Approaches in Dementia Care*. Basingstoke: Palgrave Macmillan, Chapter 11, pp. 212–230.

MacKinlay, E.B. 2001. "The Spiritual Dimension of Caring: Applying a Model for Spiritual Tasks of Aging", *Journal of Religious Gerontology*, 12, 3–4, 151–166.

Malpas, J. 2018. *Place and Experience, a Philosophical Topography, second edition*. London: Routledge.

Mathews, G., Izquierdo, C. 2009. *Pursuits of Happiness: Well-Being in Anthropological Perspective*. New York, Oxford: Berghahn Books.

Napoles, A.M., Chadiha, L., Eversley, R., Moreno-John, G. 2010. "Developing Culturally Sensitive Dementia Caregiver Interventions: Are We There Yet?" *American Journal of Alzheimer's Disease and Other Dementias*, 25, 5, 389–406.

Nicholson, P. 2018. "Family Trees, Selfies and Our Search for Identity", *The Psychologist*, November 2018. Leicester: British Psychological Society.

Reilly, S., Nolan, C., Monckton, L. 2018. Historic England, Wellbeing and Historic Environment: Why Bother? https://historicengland.org.uk/whats-new/research/wellbeing-and-the-historic-environment/.

Rothman, B.K. 2000. *Recreating Motherhood*. New York: W.W. Norton and Company.

Smith, L. 2006. *The Uses of Heritage*. London and New York: Routledge.

Suh, E.M., Koo, J. 2008. "Comparing Subjective Well-being Across Cultures and Nations: The 'What' and 'Why' Questions". *In*: Eid, M. and Larsen, R.J. (Eds.) *The Science of Subjective Well-Being*. New York: Guilford Press, pp. 414–430.

Thurgood, M., 2009. "Engaging Clients in their Care and Treatment". *In*: Norman, I. and Ryrie, I. (Eds.) *The Art and Science of Mental Health Nursing. A Textbook of Principles and Practice, Second Edition*. Berkshire: McGraw Hill, Open University Press, Chapter 27, p. 630.

Tilley, C. 1994. *A Phenomenology of Landscape Places, Paths and Monuments (Explorations in Anthropology)*. Oxford: Berg 3PL.

Todres, L. 2004. "The Wound that Connects: A Consideration of 'Narcissism' and the Creation of Soulful Space", *Indo-Pacific Journal of Phenomenology*, 4, 1, 1–12.

Todres, L. 2007. *Embodied Enquiry: Phenomenological Touchstones for Research, Psychotherapy and Spirituality*. Basingstoke: Palgrave Macmillan.

Verity, J., Lee, H. 2011. "Reigniting the Human Spirit". *In*: Less, H. and Adams, T. (Eds.) *Creative Approaches in Dementia Care*. Basingstoke: Palgrave, p. 16.

World Health Organisation (WHO). 2019. Social Determinants of Health. www.who.int/social_determinants/en/

Chapter 5

Creativity and wellbeing

Introduction

Creativity has become a fashionable and desirable attribute for people living in a contemporary culture. It is linked with excitement, attractiveness and prosperity, and can even be considered 'sexy' as demonstrated by, on average, creative people having twice the number of sexual partners as the wider population (Nettle and Clegg 2006). In 2016, the Department for Culture, Media and Sport (DCMS) in the UK reported that there were 1.9 million jobs in the creative industries. This was an increase of 19.5 per cent since 2011 despite the economic downturn and compared with a 6.3 per cent increase in the total number of jobs in the wider UK economy (DCMS 2016).

Creativity

Creativity, as with the other concepts explored within this book, is a complex phenomenon to define, leading to Plucker *et al.* (2004: 86) stating it is a "fuzzy, soft construct" which promotes mythologising, unfounded definitions and confusion. Gillam (2018) attempts to demystify creativity using several approaches including historical development, the creative state of mind, everyday creativity and radical creativity. He describes Sawyer's (2012 cited in Gillam 2018) three waves of development as:

- First wave 1950s to 1960s: creativity was considered a specific personality trait; structural definition
- Second wave 1970s to 1980s: creativity was identified as a cognitive process
- Third wave 1980s to 1990s: shift from focus on the individual to a sociocultural definition; creativity as an interactional activity and contextual

The individualistic approach of the first and second waves provides a definition which includes novelty or originality, the combination of thoughts or actions and expression in the world. Whereas the third wave offers a social dimension to the definition, it too includes novelty and something expressed in the world, but creativity in this sense provides usefulness or value to a certain social group. Using Sawyer's definition, Gillam identifies a triad of novelty, combination and expression to define creativity, but he goes on to identify other theorists that provide different triads of creativity. Cropley (2001 cited in Gillam 2018) proposes these three key aspects of creativity:

- Novelty, included by all theorists
- Effectiveness, as with Sawyer's third wave
- Ethicality, also like Sawyer's third wave including usefulness or value

Weston (2007 cited in Gillam 2018) argues that anyone can learn to be creative – a view associated with the second (cognitive) wave of creativity research. He goes on to state that creativity involves 'playfulness and discipline' and those exhibiting it are characterised by critical thinking, imagination, inventiveness, discipline and persistence. By contrast Bohm (2004 cited in Gillam 2018) recognises the importance of context and culture but states creativity cannot be learnt, it is a by-product of a *creative mind*, which sits more comfortably with the first wave of development definition of creativity. The creative mind is one that has the attribute of creativity that can be accessed to develop novel entities.

Everyday creativity and *radical creativity* from Gillam's exploration appear to include what has been labelled big c and little c. Big c, radical creativity, is where professional artists/creatives produce pieces for grand public display to create a world changing force whereas little c occurs in a more simplistic application of easily learnt techniques. Both these forms of creativity can be pragmatic and involve simple techniques, and both fall within the concept of creativity.

Gillam's (2018) exploration of the literature led him to offer the key aspects of creativity as novelty, effectiveness and ethicality, discipline and playfulness, as well as creativity as a healing, life-affirming activity. A healing and life-affirming aspect of creativity can clearly be seen in Lane's writing:

> To live creatively is to touch everything with joyful unexpected magic. It is to nourish the children's bedtime stories with fresh invention; to delight visitors with an astonishing dish served on the carefully laid table; to enrich the garden with unheard of combinations of plants; to enchant a room with decoration and colour; to paint pictures, make music, write poems, to play with life. The playful life is one intoxicated by spirit, at once unselfconscious and spontaneous, yet disciplined.
>
> (Lane 2006: 75)

This view of creativity can also be distinguished in some of the creative writing undertaken as part of the Rookwood project, as seen in Box 5.1.

Box 5.1 A poem created in response to Rookwood workshops

Green Pyjamas

A Victorian Lady called this place Rookwood
But actually, it was ebony birds in flight that bestowed the name.

I was seduced through the trees by your seclusion, your fall, your silence,
By your inconsistent lines and how they dabbled with the light –
A profusion of chinks and shafts superimposing and teasing.
A broken thing, beautiful to an eye such as mine spellbound
By your negative space laced luxuriantly with shadows of laurel, yew and lime.
Too patiently to be seen, nature was embalming you in green bandages
As I stood enamoured.
Maybe, she is granting you a stab at eternity.
The gothic vault of your bowels muttered dankly that this should be possible.
I have no doubt the walls of that chamber will outlive the outline of my years.
Indeed, you have the privilege of a preservation order.
I wonder how that feels.
However, it does not cover your un-architectured harmony –
Your stone meeting leaf, your beam meeting branch and your light meeting shadow.
Thank you for greeting me informally in your green pyjamas.

You prompted the return of my ten-year-old eyes,
And they skipped across your hidden contours – your playground just out of reach –
Marvelling at how the fencing and scaffolding
Had been absorbed into your present aesthetic.
You have relaxed towards a more organic manifestation.
The neatness of your octagonal inception has given way to a more interesting state –
A wondrous new integrity, a lounging rather than a standing.
A folly has no mission
But is designed to make a statement – a kind of ta-dah, this is me
But now there is more of a yawn and a laid back I am here in this wooded place.
I am glad I can only glimpse you through the trees, glad that I am fenced out
And that the tendrils of my imagination alone can enter.

Jane Lewis

Inspired by the Summerhouse and Vaulted Chamber, dating back to the thirteenth century, and resurrected at Rookwood Hospital. April 2019.

Creativity, the ability to use imagination and make things, is recognised as a human need and part of normal personality development by many psychologists. The American Academy of Arts and Sciences (2013: 13) states that the arts and humanities "go beyond the immediate and instrumental to help us understand the past and future … they are critical to our pursuit of life, liberty, and happiness".

There is a growing body of evidence which demonstrates the importance of creativity to develop and maintain a sense of wellbeing which has led to events in the UK such as the annual London Creativity and Wellbeing Week and the All-Party Parliamentary Group (APPG) on Arts, Health and Wellbeing. The UK is, though, not at the forefront of this movement; countries like Australia, Cuba and the Nordic countries have been extensively using creative and cultural interventions in health and wellbeing for some time (APPG 2017).

Likewise, "the idea that creative expression can make a powerful contribution to the healing process has been embraced in many different cultures. Throughout recorded history, people have used pictures, stories, dances, and chants as healing rituals" (Stuckey and Nobel 2010). Lane (2006) goes on to state that creativity is not only desirable for wellbeing, it is necessary for mental health and wellbeing to avoid burnout.

Social determinants of health and wellbeing

> The social determinants of health are the conditions in which people are born, grow, live, work and age. These circumstances are shaped by the distribution of money, power and resources at global, national and local levels. The social determinants of health are mostly responsible for health inequities – the unfair and avoidable differences in health status seen within and between countries.
>
> (WHO 2019)

The APPG (2017) agree that unequal distribution of power, income, goods and services within and between countries creates large differentials in health and wellbeing.

The APPG offer an example from the UK stating that children born into families in lower socioeconomic groups are more vulnerable to heart disease, mental health problems, obesity, respiratory disease and stroke than their more affluent contemporaries. This is of global concern (WHO 2019) but the body of evidence to support the belief that the arts have an important contribution to make to health and wellbeing is developing in scholarly work (Ramsden *et al.* 2011).

The UK is increasingly using arts-based strategies to address the social determinants of health. Whilst individuals have limited power to change their life stage, environment, sense of place and community, they are crucial to health and wellbeing. The APPG offer some examples of how these areas can be developed through engagement with the arts. They state that engagement supports mitigation of the effects of adverse environments. This can be achieved through their influence on maternal nutrition, perinatal mental health and childhood development; shaping educational and employment opportunities and tackling chronic distress; enabling self-expression and empowerment and overcoming social isolation. Embracing the arts through health and wellbeing systems can also help to overcome inequalities in access to publicly funded arts, which are mostly accessed by the educated middle class.

In all four areas of creative artistic expression they reviewed, music engagement, visual arts therapy, movement-based creative expression and expressive writing, Stuckey and Nobel (2010) found clear indications that artistic engagement significantly, positively affects health. Despite limitations the studies appeared to indicate that creative engagement can decrease anxiety, stress and mood disturbances. Creative engagement will improve psychological and physical wellbeing and quality of life. Through creativity and imagination, identity can be discovered, and individual reservoirs of healing increased. Studies within the engagement with creative visual arts review collected the following findings:

- Art filled occupational voids, distracted thoughts of illness; improvements in flow and spontaneity, expression of grief, positive identity, social networks
- Psychological variables: Improved well-being by decreasing negative emotions and increasing positive ones
- Medical outcomes, depression, dialysis times, weight gain, laboratory data
- Improved medical outcomes, trends toward reduced depression and haemodialysis parameters
- Stress, anxiety, emotions: Reductions in stress and anxiety; increases in positive emotions
- Reductions in distress and negative emotions
- Reductions in stress and symptoms of compassion fatigue; increases in healing, well-being, and sense of purpose
- Well-being: Improved focus on positive life experiences, self-worth, and social identity

(Stuckey and Nobel 2010: 257)

Dolan and Metcalfe (2012) established that creativity and subjective wellbeing are correlated but more specifically that life evaluations are associated with higher imagination and originality than the general population, measures of experience are associated with originality (happiness and having a degree), working in research and development is associated with higher evaluations of job. They do, though, caution that despite being statistically significant these are early findings in the area and causal relationships have not been found.

Much of the research conducted in the area of wellbeing is through self-report and observation; both are fraught with methodological limitations. Leckey (2011), in a systematic review of the literature of creative activities in mental health care, found the evidence for efficacy weak. This is based on the problems with the concept of mental health, wellbeing and creative activity all being rather nebulous and Leckey (2011) cites McNaught (2011: 7,8) as stating creative arts are "a complex, confusing and contested field (with) competing and contradictory definitions". Despite these problems and the need for the concepts to be clearly defined to gain rigorous high-quality research, Box 5.2 shows that Leckey's review did produce a great deal of positive low-level confidence evidence.

Box 5.2 Levels of evidence – hierarchy of research confidence

- Ia: systematic review or meta-analysis of RCTs
- Ib: at least one RCT
- IIa: at least one well-designed controlled study without randomisation
- IIb: at least one well-designed quasi-experimental study, such as a cohort study
- III: well-designed non-experimental descriptive studies, such as comparative studies, correlation studies, case-control studies and case series
- IV: expert committee reports, opinions and/or clinical experience of respected authorities

(Tidy 2014)

The evidence indicates that creative activities can have a healing and protective effect on mental wellbeing. They can facilitate relaxation, provide a means of self-expression, reduce blood pressure, boost the immune system and reduce stress. Leckey (2011) therefore concludes the potential of creative arts as a therapeutic and transformational tool is immense.

Whilst systematic reviews of the research are fraught with methodological issues, there is real-world and phenomenological evidence to support the impact of creativity. Despite this the research community continue to seek valid scientifically accepted studies. An example (MPNHSFT 2019) of a realist approach being used to evaluate participatory arts activity in relation to health and wellbeing is provided by the Be Creative Be Well project. It was orchestrated and evaluated on the basis of a theory of change – "namely, that a creative or arts-based intervention in a particular community will enable it, and the individuals within it, to achieve higher levels of wellbeing, better mental health and wider participation in the arts" (Ings *et al.* 2012: 16).

The findings from this project were that engaging in the arts can provide:

- Distraction from mental health issues
- Social interaction with other people
- Increased confidence
- Chance to learn new skills

- Renewed self-esteem
- Connections with people
- The opportunity to be treated as a person rather than a patient
- Opportunities for people to shine and discover the skills, creativity and potential they have

(MPNHSFT 2019)

Mental wellbeing has been linked in many studies to creativity and engagement in creative activities; this has also been found to occur in children and young people. Zarobe and Bungay (2017) found that participating in creative activities can have a positive effect on self-confidence, self-esteem, relationship building and a sense of belonging. These qualities have been associated with resilience and mental wellbeing (Zarobe and Bungay 2017). Posner and Patoine (2009) also found that art training improved attention and cognition.

Whilst many researchers and writer are plagued by the governmental hierarchy of evidence, as above, when attempting to develop healthcare practice and wellbeing some advocate a change in research culture. Todres *et al.* (2014) states that 'evidence' is humbled by the unique context of health care. The conventional professional discourse on evidence-based practice is an unrealistic fantasy that privileges evidence (knowledge) per se over understanding and judgement (wisdom). He advocates a process of 'reaching towards' insiderness through phenomenologically informed insights to develop practice, with reaching towards suggesting a process or productive direction rather than a completed achievement (Todres *et al.* 2014). Knowledge offers general understanding of 'insiderness' or the lived experience but does not open the practitioner to openness to the nuanced encounters that patients may provide.

Flourishing is mentioned in this book in several places and is considered from both a positivist and idiopathic approach. The following is mostly positivist given the requirements of healthcare but it provides a robust rationale for further research, particularly to develop understanding.

Flourishing

Tay *et al.* (2018) believe that creative arts and humanities may also strengthen aspects of human flourishing, such as character, values, civic engagement and morality. They offer a conceptual framework for the role of the arts and humanities in human flourishing. It consists of the 'what' and 'how' of the art or humanity and the mechanisms that lead to human flourishing outcomes. The 'what' or extensional definition objects include disciplines, occupations, topics and courses. The 'how' or functional analysis subjects include modes of engagement and activities of involvement. The mechanisms that mediate the how and what achieving flourishing outcomes are immersion, embeddedness, socialisation and reflectiveness, and an example of this framework is in Box 5.3.

Box 5.3 Application of conceptual model to an experience of the Collingwood project

I attended a series of workshops [*the what/extensional definition*] as part of an exploration of the recently acquired Collingwood Archive. The archivist helped me to find artefacts that I was interested in [*the how/functional analysis*]. I loved looking at the small pictures drawn and painted by the Collingwood children and I felt a longing to able to draw and paint pictures like this myself [*immersion*]. I particularly liked Ursula's little cat and bird pictures. The archivist told me more about Ursula [*the how/functional analysis*] and I became even more interested in her creative work because she sounded as if she was someone I would like to be similar to or to meet.

In the workshop I was supported to use pencils and watercolours to create a small booklet [*the how/functional analysis*] similar to the ones I had seen that the children had done. I became quite engrossed *[embeddedness]* in the moment and the time whizzed by, I found myself smiling at my work [*creativity, affect valence*] even though it was not as good as the children's! As I drove home I found I was still smiling and thinking about sitting in a pretty parlour with Edwardian clothes on like Ursula or under a summer shade in the painting place they used by the lake [*subjective wellbeing*].

Tay *et al.* (2018) identify four areas of human flourishing in their framework:

- Neurological/physiological/psychological reactions
    - Activation of brain areas
    - Cardiovascular, endocrine, immune
    - Affect valence
- Psychological competencies
    - Self-efficacy
    - Integrative complexity
    - Creativity
- General wellbeing effects
    - Subjective wellbeing
    - Psychological wellbeing
    - Physical wellbeing
- Positive normative outcomes
    - Character/virtues
    - Ethical choices
    - Moral compass
    - Civic engagement

As identified above creativity can be learnt using techniques or nurturing of a state of mind; it can be an everyday activity or special and radical. Weston

(2007), who states creativity is 'a way of life', offers methods for promoting creativity:

- Association – provision of random words, images or other prompts
- Interaction – talking to other people, sharing views and ideas
- Analysis – compare historical and cultural examples
- Challenge – exaggerate a feature and push it as far as possible
- Combine – mix and match things not originally experienced together

(Adapted from Weston 2007)

If a nurse has "no belief, no commitment, no delight" in their work (Lane 2006: 75) it is likely they also have little compassion left either. Whilst the importance of having a job is undeniable in an economic financial sense, what leads to 'progress', 'life's further development' and constitutes a 'good life' is human relationships and meaning (Seligman 2002; Forgeard *et al.* 2011). As Halpern (2010) highlights, it is relationships that make our societies and these are the 'hidden wealth'. This hidden wealth has a big impact on wellbeing and the meaning we attribute to relationships. It is undeniable that the creative arts are intimately involved in meaning-making, through their practices (activities) and interactions with the artefacts that are consequently developed. These both provide connections and meaning (Wright and Pascoe 2015).

Eudaemonia, sometimes defined as wellbeing or happiness, is dynamic, culturally defined and determined (involves relationships with others), is where artistry and learning are profoundly intertwined and what is felt or sensate is always present. Eudaemonia focuses on individuals' meaningful engagement in life, their self-realisation (Ryan and Deci, 2001), and in this way, both being and becoming, pleasure and process are linked in terms of *flourishing* (Geurts and Adikha 2006). As outlined, Tay *et al.*'s (2018) framework on human flourishing demonstrates how creativity links to wellbeing through the mechanisms of immersion, embeddedness, socialisation and reflectiveness, providing a framework for future research. This is similar to the relational, self-realisation and meaningful engagement of Ryan and Deci, and Geurts and Adikha, through a 'felt sense' to develop eudaemonia.

Five paths to wellbeing framework

The Five Ways to Wellbeing were developed by the New Economics Foundation (NEF) who were commissioned by Foresight (the UK government's futures think-tank) (Foresight 2008). This framework has been widely used within healthcare but also the arts and humanities, particularly Historic England (Reilly *et al.* 2018). The five paths to wellbeing are in Table 5.1.

Table 5.1 Five ways to wellbeing linked to art and creativity

	The five ways to wellbeing	*Linked to art and creativity*
1	Connect ...with other people in various contexts and invest time in them	Undertake a group activity to meet people with similar interests
2	Be active ...undertake some physical activity that brings some pleasure	Walk in the countryside, garden, dance, act
3	Take notice ...Be curious	See something beautiful, a picture, an animal, landscape
4	Keep learning ...Try something new, set a challenge	Undertake a creative workshop such as watercolours, weaving
5	Give ...Do something nice for another person, thank someone, smile	Volunteer, share your creativity with others

Arts practice and creativity can facilitate the achievement of the five ways to wellbeing; as already established it involves team-work, perseverance, imagination and discipline. They also allow the deepening understanding of diverse concepts and support building of identity.

Awakening understanding and creative ways of thinking promotes a hidden wealth of experiences of self, others and culture. These offer interdependency and recognition of unrealised creative futures, filling life with engagement, meaning, relationships and a fuller humanity (Wright and Pascoe 2015).

Carl Rogers, one of the founding fathers of humanistic psychology, was said to be the first to promote psychotherapy research as he sought an evidence base for his therapeutic interactions. His humanistic approach put the troubled person at the centre, recognising their knowledge and understanding of themselves was the best remedy for them to psychologically move on. His approach was said to be non-interventional, but he did manage the therapeutic environment and their relationship. His daughter, Natalie Rogers, was to build on this using a feminist creative approach.

Natalie Rogers, the founder of person-centred expressive arts, offers the conditions for creativity based on the foundational theory developed by him. Rogers (1993: 14) states:

> The Conditions that foster creativity
>
> 1 Psychological safety
>   a Accepting the individual as of unconditional worth
>   b Providing a climate in which external evaluation is absent
>   c Understanding empathetically
> 2 Psychological freedom
> 3 Offering stimulating and challenging experiences

Before the instigation of evidence-based practice, arts and creative activities were being used within health services, particularly mental health services. One way in which this has been developed is through art therapy.

Art as therapy

Art therapy was formally initiated in the UK in the 1940s in the National Health Service and is regulated by the British Association of Art Therapists (BAAT) but drawing and painting have been recognised as being therapeutic for some time before this (BAAT 2019). It is used within psychiatric, psychological and neurological health services.

Art therapy involves creative activity and art-making processes targeting cognitive, motor, emotional and interpersonal skills. It serves as a non-verbal expressive medium, which offers insights into the 'inner world' through a three-way process between the person, the therapist and art materials (object or image) (BAAT 2019).

Some authors differentiate between art as treatment and art as an activity, but it is frequently seen as a holistic approach to the person's recovery. It is recognised that art activities can promote wellbeing alongside the therapeutic interaction between the person and the therapist.

Box 5.4 Art as an activity – part of a reflection from the Rookwood workshops

When I started the workshops, I didn't realise just how important taking part would be and how it would make me feel … what it would be like to experience being on 'the other side' receiving guidance on printmaking techniques. How would it make me feel to leave my ego outside (after all I came from a printmaking background and should know a lot about this) and wipe the slate clean to try something new? …

One of the processes produced sophisticated results, yet it was surprisingly simple to achieve … all it needed was space and a bit of time. Could I make something as beautiful as that? …

Hidden illnesses and a chance encounter had brought us together. Anxiety, depression, phobias, creative blocks … how could taking part do anything to shift these feelings and put us on a different path? …

Once it had all come to an end, the sense of achievement and positivity did enhance the way I felt. It felt great that I had taken time out for myself, guilt-free to release those feelings of being stuck.…

Art therapy has all the complexity and confusion over definition and explanation as the concepts already discussed here, but Huss (2009: 154) describes it as "dynamic, humanistic, systemic-social understandings of art, therapy, and people". Huss identified how art therapy can be conceptualised through all psychological and cultural perspectives. Each theoretical model tends to focus on the process and context of art activities, or art as an analytical tool. Huss' multi-layered model has been developed to integrate the different theoretical conceptualisations, allowing each prism to add to the engagement, intervention and understanding of the areas of concern for the person (2017).

Box 5.5 Art as treatment – part of a reflection from Collingwood workshops

I arrived in a rush … late again! I started apologising and stumbling over my words. Louise was great; she encouraged me to get myself a hot drink and sit down. She organised the others and then came, sat by my side and smiled. I was starting to feel better, a drink and person with time to listen and attend to me. She asked me if I'd like to talk. I looked down and shook my head. How could I tell her of the awful things that had been happening? What words could I use?

Louise explained we were going to make some small booklets like the ones we had seen the Collingwood children make. They were pretty and sweet with little birds, animals and flowers. I was not an artist; I couldn't do beautiful things like that. She encouraged me to choose a simple picture that I liked – I chose the cat – and talked to me about why I liked it, what it represented for me. She listened to me as if what I said mattered and that I was worth listening to – it was as if I was worth something – in that moment I did matter. I realised the little cat was demonstrating where and what I wanted to be. It was small, pretty and made me want to nurse it – to love it. Whilst thinking about what the little picture meant to me Louise left me trying to copy it. Despite my lack of drawing skills my anxiety gradually reduced, and I was able to focus on something pretty, delicate and feminine which allowed me to feel more acceptable in myself.

Art for health interventions are usually based in primary care in the UK as a form of social prescribing. This allows patients to be referred to non-clinical services who were using primary services excessively, due to poor mental health, family problems or lack of support or a number of these. These services have been found to be effective in the promotion of wellbeing and engaging with people from lower socioeconomic groups (Crone *et al.* 2013). Many of the Art for Health interventions are supported by charities and volunteers but are still part of social prescribing.

Social prescribing

Social prescribing, sometimes referred to as community referral, is a means of enabling GPs, nurses and other primary care professionals to refer people to a range of local, non-clinical services. Social prescribing is based on the recognition that health and wellbeing are determined by a range of social, economic and environmental factors (see social determinants of health earlier in this chapter). It is said to address people's health and wellbeing needs in a holistic way and aims to support individuals to take greater control of their wellbeing.

Whilst social prescribing has become more acceptable the schemes differ in each geographical area. Most of them are provided by voluntary and community sector organisations. Examples include volunteering, arts activities, group learning, gardening, befriending, cookery, healthy eating advice and a range of sports. The different models usually involve a link worker who works with people to enable their access to local sources of support.

The components of social prescribing usually include:

1 Shared decision making
2 Personalised care and support planning
3 Enabling choice, including legal rights to choice
4 Social prescribing and community-based support
5 Supported self-management
6 Personal health budgets and integrated personal budgets

(NHS England 2019)

Despite social prescribing becoming widely popular in the UK, the evidence base for it is quite limited. As with arts, creativity and history, many of the studies are small and do not have a control group, nor are they related to individual interventions. The research is mostly qualitative and/or relies on self-report which makes drawing generalisable conclusions a challenge between different schemes, particularly when the complexity of the interventions is considered (The Kings Fund 2019).

There is, though, growing evidence that social prescribing is effective from similar pilot projects undertaken in the UK after 18–24 months of intervention. Outcomes include:

- Improved health and quality of life
- Increased patient satisfaction
- Fewer primary care consultations
- Reductions in the number of hospital admissions, visits to Accident and Emergency, and outpatient attendances
- Decrease in the use of wider hospital resources

(Rotherham Social Prescribing Project 2014)

The expansion to date of the evidence base in the field of arts, health and wellbeing is encouraging. There are health and wellbeing benefits of arts engagement but more needs to be done to consolidate the evidence base, perhaps especially in relation to the social determinants of health (APPG 2017). Social prescribing as part of statutory services provides models and frameworks which should facilitate more rigorous high-quality research to provide a robust evidence base for the use of arts in wellbeing. Whilst this will encourage service providers to feel secure in their decision making, further exploration which considers its impact on the wider society and culture needs to be considered.

Summary

At the beginning of this chapter creativity as a concept was explored. Initially it was identified that it can be considered a 'fuzzy soft concept' but at the same time sexy. It was recognised that despite there being a number of descriptions of creativity, with many psychologists agreeing creativity is to do with the ability to use the imagination and make things, it is recognised as a human need and part of normal personality development. Lane (2006) goes on to state that creativity is not only desirable for wellbeing, it is necessary for mental health and wellbeing to avoid burnout.

To try to unpack the evidence base for the efficacy of creativity, social determinants of health and wellbeing were explored to understand what the current situation is and what is hoped for. The evidence indicates that creative activities can have a healing and protective effect on mental wellbeing but there are limitations to the current evidence base.

Mental wellbeing was examined in previous chapters and it was found that wellbeing and flourishing can be used interchangeably. Flourishing offers another perspective on the aims for creativity and wellbeing. Tay *et al.* (2018) offer a framework to research flourishing which is a detailed psychological exploration whereas NEF's (Foresight 2008) five paths to wellbeing offer a very pragmatic approach focused on change.

The chapter finished by considering the theory of Carl Rogers and his daughter who provided healthcare workers and psychologists with guidance on how to manage the therapeutic relationship. This led to consideration of how an understanding of the impact of creativity in wellbeing could be put into practice. Art therapy has been accepted within health care for decades to support wellbeing despite the limited evidence base, and more recently social prescribing has been incorporated into statutory services, again with limited evidence.

References

All-Party Parliamentary Group on Arts, Health and Wellbeing (APPG). 2017. Creative Health: The Arts for Health and Wellbeing, Second Edition. London: APPG.

American Academy of Arts and Sciences. 2013. Humanities Report Card. Retrieved from: www.amacad.org/binaries/hum_report_card.pdf.

British Association of Art Therapists. 2019. www.baat.org/.

Crone, D.M., O'Connell, E.E., Tyson, P.J., Clarke-Stone, F., Opher, S., James, D.V.B. 2013. "'Art Lift' Intervention to Improve Mental Wellbeing: An Observational Study from UK General Practice", *International Journal of Mental Health Nursing* (2013), 22, 279–286.

Department for Culture, Media and Sport. 2016. Creative Industries: Focus on Employment, June 2016. London: Department for Culture, Media and Sport.

Retrieved from: https://assets.publishing.service.gov.uk/government/uploads/system/uploads/attachment_data/file/534305/Focus_on_Employment_revised_040716.pdf.

Dolan, P., Metcalfe, R. 2012. "The Relationship Between Innovation and Subjective Wellbeing", *Research Policy*, 41, 1489–1498.

Foresight. 2008. Foresight Mental Capital and Wellbeing Project: Final Project Report. London: The Government Office for Science. Retrieved from: https://assets.publishing.service.gov.uk/government/uploads/system/uploads/attachment_data/file/292453/mental-capital-wellbeing-summary.pdf.

Forgeard, M.J.C., Jayawickreme, E., Kern, M.L., Seligman, M.E.P. 2011. "Doing the Right Thing: Measuring Wellbeing for Public Policy", *International Journal of Wellbeing*, 1, 79–106.

Geurts, K.L., Adikha, E.G. 2006. "Enduring and Endearing Feelings and the Transformation of Material Culture in West Africa". *In*: Edwards, E., Gosden, C. and Phillips, R.B. (Eds.) *Sensible Objects: Colonialism, Museums and Material Culture*. Oxford: Berg, pp. 35–60.

Gillam, T. 2018. *Creativity, Wellbeing and Mental Health Practice*. Basingstoke: Palgrave.

Halpern, D. 2010. *The Hidden Wealth of Nations*. Cambridge: Polity Press.

Huss, E. 2009. "'A Coat of Many Colors.' Towards an Integrative Multi-layered Model of Art Therapy", *The Arts in Psychotherapy*, 36, 154–160.

Huss, E. 2017. *A Theory-based Approach to Art Therapy: Implications for Teaching, Research and Practice*. London: Routledge.

Ings, R., Crane, N., Cameron, M. 2012. Be Creative Be Well: Arts, Wellbeing and Local Communities, an Evaluation. The Arts Council England, p. 16.

Lane, J. 2006. *The Spirit of Silence: Making Space for Creativity*. Totnes: Green Books, p. 75.

Leckey, J. 2011. "The Therapeutic Effectiveness of Creative Activities on Mental Well-being: A Systematic Review of the Literature", *Journal of Psychiatric and Mental Health Nursing*, 18, 6, 501–509.

McNaught, A. (2011). "Defining Wellbeing". *In*: Knight, A. and McNaught, A. (Eds.) *Understanding Wellbeing: An Introduction for Students and Practitioners of Health and Social Care*. Banbury: Lantern Publishing Limited, pp. 7–8.

Midlands Partnership NHS Foundation Trust (MPNHSFT). 2019. Arts for Health. https://artsforhealth.mpft.nhs.uk/.

Nettle, D., Clegg, H. 2006. "Schizotypy, Creativity and Mating Success in Humans", *Proceedings of the Royal Society of London B: Biological Sciences*, 273, 611–615.

NHS England. 2019. Social Prescribing. www.england.nhs.uk/wp-content/uploads/2019/01/social-prescribing-community-based-support-summary-guide.pdf.

Plucker, J.A., Beghetto, R.A., Dow, G.T. 2004. "Why Isn't Creativity More Important to Educational Psychologists? Potentials, Pitfalls, and Future Directions in Creativity Research", *Educational Psychologist*, 39, 2, 83–96.

Posner, M.I., Patoine, B. 2009. How Arts Training Improves Attention and Cognition. Cerebrum. Retrieved from: www.dana.org/article/how-arts-training-improves-attention-and-cognition/.

Ramsden, H., Milling, J., Phillimore, J., McCabe, Fyfe, H. *et al*. 2011. The Role of Grassroots Arts Activities in Communities: A Scoping Study. Third Sector Research Centre Working Paper 68.

Reilly, S., Nolan, C. and Monkton, L. 2018. Historic England, Wellbeing and the Historic Environment: Why Bother? https://historicengland.org.uk/whats-new/research/wellbeing-and-the-historic-environment/.

Rogers, N. 1993. *The Creative Connection. Expressive Arts in Healing.* California: Science and Behaviour Books Inc.

Rotherham Social Prescribing Project. 2014. www4.shu.ac.uk/research/cresr/sites/shu.ac.uk/files/social-economic-impact-rotherham.pdf.

Ryan, R.M., Deci, E.L. 2001. "On Happiness and Human Potentials: A Review of Research on Hedonic and Eudaimonic Well-being", *Annual Review of Psychology*, 52, 141–166. DOI: https://doi.org/10.1146/annurev.psych.52.1.141.

Seligman, M.E.P. 2002. *Authentic Happiness: Using the New Positive Psychology to Realize Your Potential for Lasting Fulfillment.* New York: Free Press.

Stuckey, H.L., Nobel, J. 2010. "The Connection between Art, Healing, and Public Health: A Review of Current Literature", *American Journal of Public Health*, 100, 2, 254–261. DOI: 10.2105/AJPH.2008.156497. Available at: www.ncbi.nlm.nih.gov/pmc/articles/PMC2804629/#bib27.

Tay, L., Pawelski, J.O., Keith, M.K. 2018. "The Role of the Arts and Humanities in Human Flourishing: A Conceptual Model", *The Journal of Positive Psychology*, 13, 3, 215–225. DOI: 10.1080/17439760.2017.1279207.

The Kings Fund. 2019. Social Prescribing. www.kingsfund.org.uk/publications/social-prescribing.

Tidy, C. 2014. Level of Evidence through NICE Portal. https://patient.info/doctor/different-levels-of-evidence#nav-2.

Todres, L., Galvin, K.T., Dahlberg, K. 2014 "'Caring for Insiderness': Phenomenologically Informed Insights that Can Guide Practice", *International Journal of Qualitative Studies on Health and Well-being*, 2014, 9, 21421. DOI: http://dx.doi.org/10.3402/qhw.v9.21421.

Weston, A. 2007. *Creativity for Critical Thinkers.* New York: Oxford University Press.

World Health Organisation. 2019. About Social Determinants of Health. www.who.int/social_determinants/sdh_definition/en/.

Wright, P.R., Robin Pascoe, R. 2015. "Eudaimonia and Creativity: The Art of Human Flourishing", *Cambridge Journal of Education*, 45, 3, 295–306. DOI: 10.1080/0305764X.2013.855172.

Zarobe, L., Bungay, H. 2017. "The Role of Arts Activities in Developing Resilience and Mental Wellbeing in Children and Young People: A Rapid Review of the Literature", *Perspectives in Public Health*, 137, 6, 337–347. DOI: 10.1177/1757913917712283.

Chapter 6

Stiwdio Arts Group

Introduction

Louise Jensen is the project lead for the Stiwdio Arts Group. She has a background in the arts and in education, and an interest in the relationship between learning, creativity and wellbeing. In January 2016 she conceived the notion of the Stiwdio Arts Project. The project was born out of a wish to offer a safe and creative environment in which to quietly share a process of learning through art, developing resilience and mental wellbeing in a creative way.

Armed with a small amount of money raised from the GoFundMe webpages, Louise ran the pilot project 'Words and Images' in May 2016 in collaboration with two other practitioners in a local community centre. Since then she has developed a number of participatory Arts for Wellbeing projects which encourage inclusion and participation in project-based, creative processes. The groups offer a non-judgemental and safe environment with the aim for people to gain confidence, learn new skills and express themselves creatively. The group welcomes collaboration with other community groups and organisations, as well as with other artists, wishing to share their work and skills in this context.

Recent collaborations include projects with Cardiff University Community Gateway Project, 4Winds Mental Health Drop-In centre, Cardiff and Vale Action for Mental Health, Grangetown Community Association and Cardiff University Special Collections. The last project, which took place in Rookwood Hospital in Llandaff, Cardiff was funded and supported by the Cardiff and Vale Health Charity.

Words and images

The first project for the Stiwdio Arts Group ran over a three-week period in May 2016.

Louise set up the pilot project, 'Words and Images', and approached Alison Harvey, Special Collections at Cardiff University Library to ask if she could bring a small group of people to the archives to have a look at some of their illustrated works of poetry, as a stimulus for three day-long creative arts sessions.

It was decided that the group would look at a collection of illustrated poetry from different periods, including the work of the artist Ron King, who had donated a large collection of his book art to the archive. His pieces in particular would prove to be a great inspiration for their work and helped set the task for the group: to create their own pieces of writing and book art. Working alongside Susan Morgan, writer and lecturer at Cardiff University, and Andrea Morse, a community artist, the pilot project took place in May 2016 and ran over a period of three weeks. During this time the group met for two full days a week. They worked intensively on writing and visual arts, with different people leading each part of the programme.

The project was featured in the local media and proved to be an extremely successful collaborative venture involving a mental health organisation, taking place in Cathays, an area identified for urban development, with sixteen participants in total. This was so well evaluated that further funding was sought by the Cardiff's open-access mental health resource 4Winds alongside the Cardiff University's Community Gateway Project. The aim was to host a series of Stiwdio Arts Group workshops in the Grange Gardens Pavilion (a venue which was the hub of the university's project), to be funded by Cardiff Council's Neighbourhood Partnership Grant.

Figure 6.1 Louise, Susan and Sue at workshop.

The bee project

In July 2016 the Community Gateway Project funded a small pilot bee project which ran for three afternoons over three weeks. The group made watercolour pictures and ceramic tiles inspired by the pollinating garden which had been planted within the grounds of the Grange Gardens Pavilion. September 2016 saw funding secured from the Neighbourhood Partnership Grant and a further twelve workshops focused on the solitary bee and the importance of pollination. Louise worked with Anna Carlisle as creative lead on the project and again, the subject matter was explored through a number of different visual processes: print, ceramics and sculpture with wood. This project ran over a period of six months. There was a core group of participants from different genders, whilst some participants joined for a few sessions and then moved on.

Sharing

As was described in Chapter 5, most definitions of creativity involve novelty, combination and sharing. The participants were proud to exhibit their creations in the spring of 2017 at a local event and in the following autumn they were displayed in the Hearth Gallery in Llandough Hospital.

Portraits

The next project the Stiwdio Arts Group undertook was in February 2017.

Figure 6.2 Exhibition of bees and their hotels.

Figure 6.3 Portraits.

Cardiff and Vale Action for Mental Health were offering some funding as part of their training programme for a number of arts workshops to be delivered to their service users. Taking the theme of 'Portraits', Louise invited artists Mary Jones and Anna Carlisle to collaborate on the sessions. Mary ran a session on ceramic portraits, talking about her own work and then leading the group in a practical workshop to make their own portraits. These were glazed and later fired by Mary.

The second workshop was led by Anna Carlisle who explored charcoal drawing and collage portraits with the group.

Figure 6.4 Model of head.

Many of the people taking part in these sessions were new to the Stiwdio Arts Group, and the group numbered around nine for each of the workshops. The resulting artworks from these sessions were exhibited alongside other 'solitary bee work' in March 2017.

'Artists in the making': Collingwood project

It was on the back of these experiences, then, that in August 2017 Louise was invited back by the archivists at the Cardiff University Special Collection and Archives to see if the Stiwdio Arts Group might wish to engage with a new part of their collection. The archives had recently acquired a collection of treasures from the Collingwood family which included a wide variety of unique materials, including rare signed books dating from the sixteenth century, thousands of postcards, legal documents, photographs, sketches, paintings, thousands of letters dating from the eighteenth century, and diaries spanning three centuries.

A meeting was held with the archivist managing the collection to discuss how the group could best make use of it and what contact was permitted. It was decided that a pilot should be undertaken in the same urban area but also to a wider population than previously to check if the community would find it inspirational. There was some very positive feedback and some real curiosity in Robin Collingwood's little notelets, which had been used as a trigger mechanism.

Once a desire to work with the materials was established the parameters needed to be set as to how to approach the vast amount of source material in the archives, as well as deciding on the lens through which it would be viewed. It would be impossible and unproductive for us to trawl through all the archive material in a random way, so a focus and a task was necessary.

The previous 'Words and Images' project had worked well, and the participants appeared to have been happy with the way they had been run. Following the same format, then, the workshops would run on three separate day-long workshops over a period of three weeks. This would allow an opportunity to view the items in the collection, digest what had been seen and work creatively with them as an inspiration for the creative tasks undertaken.

Choosing the focus was an important part of the process. In order to tap into the wealth of this extraordinary family, the important thing to do would be to choose one moment in their history, a moment when the family would be in focus, a prism through which could be seen the refracted light that shone through them to gain a new understanding of them and ourselves through them.

As Louise was being introduced to the material, she was particularly drawn to the sketchbooks of the Collingwood family with William and Edith at the family's head circa 1880s. She found some beautiful pages in which Edith had taken each of her children's drawings, over a number of years, and kept a record of what they had done. This started from when the children were as young as four. She had noted down the small developments she could see in their work, pointing to what they needed to work on further. These documents were a wonderful window into the whole culture of their family life and creative work.

Louise felt, looking at this collection, that she might gain a strong sense of Edith as both mother and teacher. She said that if Edith were to speak to her today that she believed that one of the things Edith would say would be that in every child there is an artist.

The collection is filled with paintings, little storybooks, sketchbooks and drawings from all the children: Barbara, Dora, Robin and Ursula. They were prolific in their output and in some shape or form every one of them later grew into an artist, perceived as such and encouraged by Edith from the outset. In Robin's autobiography he wrote of how artists regularly came and worked at their house, and how as children they were surrounded by art. For him, growing up in that environment furnished him with the understanding that every piece of work was a work in progress, not necessarily finished, but rather, that each painting, or drawing, was an ongoing problem to solve.

It became clear to Louise at this stage that the particular moment in this family's history was the moment of their 'coming into being' as artists, spanning from the children's infancy to the years when they were all in their thirties and were already making their way in the world. She would call the project 'Artists

Figure 6.5 Watercolours.

in the Making'. This notion of 'making' was central to the group workshops, central to Louise's journey as an artist, and it had featured significantly in Robin's academic work. He was the one who reflected on the work they did as they grew up and articulated it intellectually. He wrote about the importance of action and activity, and that being an artist and working artistically was a practical question of setting to and grappling with the very real business of working with the material in hand, solving the problems.

In readiness for the project Louise set out to find the vehicle through which the group could work. Pencil, ink and watercolour were the mediums most favoured by all the Collingwood family, and Edith herself had been a successful and respected miniaturist in her time. Louise offered the notion of making miniature accordion books, with the hope that the group would create little repositories for their responses to the family members and a collection of visual notes of their characters. Each book would focus on one member of the family.

This, then, was the scaffolding that would support the way through the wealth of information set before the group. It was their artistic task.

Delivery

Day one

As members of the group, the first day was simply a visit to the archives and the collection with Judith Dray as the guide through the items previously selected (a moment in time) by her and Louise. She introduced the group to the family, one by one, and helped open up ways of seeing each member.

From the outset, Judith, as the project archivist, played a significant role in the exploration. For her, each of the family members was a fully rounded person. She called them each by their first names. She had spent hours already working through their letters, diaries, notes and annotations, getting to know them through their own writings and drawings, as well as from the way they wrote to each other, and referred to each other. Judith was, throughout the project, a rich source of information for the group, not least because she carried with her a sense of this family as being very real, present and human, with their unique idiosyncrasies, foibles, talents and concerns.

The group left the Reading Room at the archives somewhat exhausted from taking in so much information, armed with lots of photocopies of documents and images as we were not allowed to remove any of the archives. The copies taken were those that had begun to excite us and to which we could later refer and respond.

At this point we busily started talking about who we were interested in and why, and what might be achievable with the limited abilities. We worked on the covers and the structure of miniature accordion books and had a play with watercolours, setting tiny little windows to do ink and watercolour

Figure 6.6 Small pictures for Collingwood.

sketches based on our ideas of who they were and what our work could show. Judith read extracts from selected writings from each family member and the group jotted down what it was they knew about them.

Louise told the group of Robin's notions of art being a process of solving problems, and so the group set out to solve, to understand the mediums we were using instead of being self-critical of our artistic skills. We investigated watercolours, in a gentle way to begin with, to get to know their qualities and how to work with them.

We all had a go at what the children were clearly asked to do time and time again. Referring to their examples of drawings and paintings of Coniston Lake, the brooding stretch of water which lay at the bottom of their garden, we each did our own versions, putting ourselves in the shoes of the Collingwood children. One of Barbara's drawings at the age of four shows a little scene which she called 'Tea at the painting place', offering up a beautiful insight into the way they spent their days and how the activity of painting was an integral part. The 'Painting place' was a spot of grass next to the lake, ideal for drawing and painting the view.

We decided to just start working in watercolour, imagining ourselves at the 'Painting place' studying the various pictures of the lake drawn by the children, to help us produce our own.

The notion of 'making', giving it a try, was central to our project, and features significantly in Robin's work. He wrote about the importance of action and activity, and that being an artist and working artistically was a practical question of setting to and grappling with the very real business of working with the material in hand.

At the end of the workshop, we all appeared tired but content. What we could say we had learnt was … "painting with watercolours is very difficult"!

Day two

We continued by exploring the water element of watercolour, dampening our paper, and creating monoprints by splashing colour on to the paper and seeing how they turned out. These were left to dry as we then turned our attention to the business of ink pen.

The group worked to produce little pictures within a tiny space, using pen and a little watercolour to capture little notes on their chosen family member. These would later furnish the pages of the miniature books. It was during this session in particular that the group was at its most quiet, working away in concentration, channelling what we had seen so far of these people and doing what the Collingwoods did before them, just drawing, committing to paper, a moment's observation, for here, for now.

This working to produce, without allowing the judgemental side of our brain to play too big a part, was central to the way of working identified by Robin Collingwood and became our focus. At each point, Louise stressed that this was all work in progress, in the hope of releasing as much 'play' as possible. And so, we were well on with the project, the books were coming together, we had lots of material gathered, plenty to decorate the pages of our books, and each of the members of the group were beginning to show their own creative strengths.

Figure 6.7 Workshop.

At this point Louise began to ask herself,

> What did we now know of these members of the Collingwood family? How could we bring that into sharper focus for us as a group, so that we could begin to share together, out loud, what we had we learnt about them?

Going back to the pictures, and planning the day three workshop, Louise was very drawn to Edith and her related documents, which tell how she enabled the children, and herself, to develop as artists. There were some beautiful pages in which Edith had taken each of the children's drawings, noting down the small developments she could see in their work, pointing to what needed to be worked on further. These documents are a wonderful window into the whole culture of their family life and creative work. Edith gave enormous status to the children's work by doing this. The group discussed the status that was given to the children's art, at a time when they would have understood the culture to have been 'Children should be seen but not heard'.

Day three

The day began by hearing from Judith some personal words from each member of the family, from a letter, a journal, or other document, and jotted down as we went, words which came to our minds about each one. We placed the family in 1922, on December 6, and made an educated guess as to

Figure 6.8 Where were the Collingwoods?

where they would have been at that point in time. To draw the focus in even more sharply, a seventh person was introduced into the room, whom we named Maud. She was a fictional character of our own, a servant living at Coniston at the time, only a year in post, talking to her brother during a well-earned afternoon off, about the family, telling him what she knew and what she thought about each of the Collingwoods.

The exercise 'What Maud Thought' produced a distillation of what the group had come to know about the family members and was an opportunity to add another dimension to our thinking about the Collingwoods. We had become increasingly aware, as the project went on, that they were a privileged family, of a very particular class and it was a chance to add this into the mix. It was a quick-fire rendering of Maud's view of the family members, and yet stands as testament to much of what we had learnt over the three days, her words sitting happily beside our pictures of the lake, the miniature books, our splodgy watercolours and beautiful play with ink.

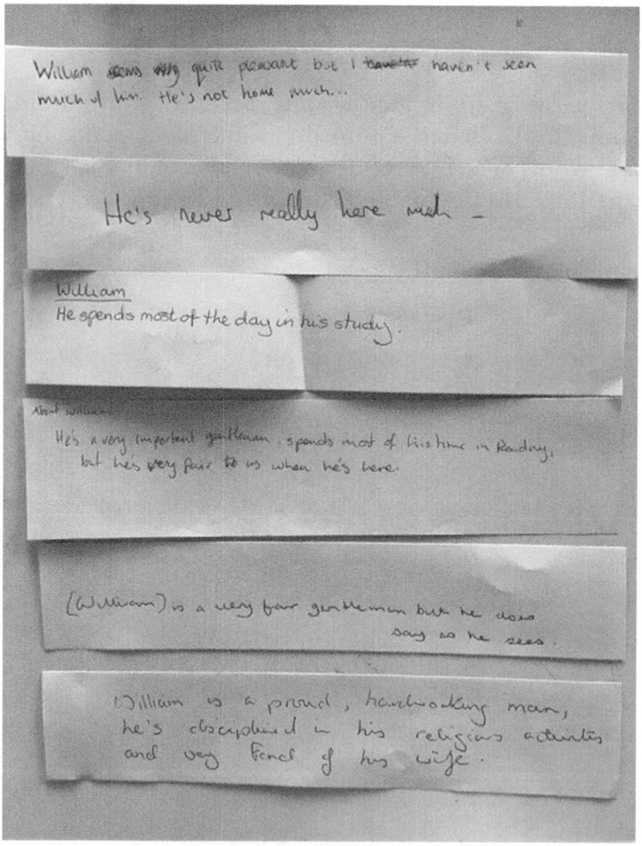

Figure 6.9 'What Maud Said' snippets.

We had come to know the Collingwood family a little better, and we had certainly got a sense of their work and who they were. Judith had given us some lovely, rather intimate insights along the way, but we needed to somehow distil further what we knew. The little books with their portraits spoke about the people, but there was still a sense of us being distanced from them, whether it was because of how far back in time they lived, or whether it was the class that they belonged to. In order to express what we knew about them, but in a slightly different way, we did a very quick creative writing exercise that no one expected. The group were introduced to Maud. She was inspired by the little drawing of the servant in the corner of Edith's housekeeping notes.

Maud, employed by the Collingwoods only a year, was enjoying an afternoon's visit from her brother Albert, and telling him all about the family. We were invited to imagine what she might have said to him, about each member of the family in one quick sentence. Our responses were then quickly edited together, and these formed the basis of 'What Maud Said' which can be found in Box 6.1.

Box 6.1 'What Maud Said' – A Flight of Fancy

ALBERT: So tell me everything! What is the family like? What is Mr Collingwood like?

MAUD: Well. He seems quite pleasant, but I haven't seen much of him. He lives in Reading most of the time you know. Lecturing. He's meant to be coming home any day now, though, for Christmas. He's a very fair gentleman, says as he sees, you know. He's proud, hardworking, disciplined in his religious activity and very fond of his wife.

ALBERT: His wife, is that Edith?

MAUD: Ooh yes, Edith, she is a perfectionist, she likes things to be just so. She does love her children, but she's strict with them as well. She's very easy to work for in a way. There's no mistake about what she wants, she's got us as well behaved as that little dog of theirs.

ALBERT: And what about the son? Did you say he's a writer?

MAUD: Blimey, what a man! Very serious, always looks intense and brooding. Very intelligent man. He lectures at Oxford. Very studious. I see his office lit up all hours of the day and night when he's back at home. Bit of a night owl.

ALBERT: So, is he the youngest of the four of them? Oh no, you said that was Ursula? The midwife who works in London?

MAUD: Yes, oh I like Ursula, I miss her when she's away. She stands up for us working folk. She's on the go all of the time, no stopping her. She's over the other side of the world, as we speak, patching people up. She's visiting Dora at the moment doing her Christian duty for the poor people in Aleppo. She's a hardworking person caring for others, delivering babies. … She's got very strong opinions too.

ALBERT: So, she does painting you say, is she the one that does all the sculpting too?

MAUD: No, that's Barbara. She's very good with her hands, carving out people's faces that look so real, you could mistake that they were here. Jolly woman. Lives in London and I think she has admirers, but she spends all her time sculpting naked people.

ALBERT: Oh! Is she married?

MAUD: No, her mother keeps trying to marry her off to any gentleman that comes to the village, but she knows her own mind. She won't settle for any Tom, Dick or Harry …

ALBERT: So that just leaves the eldest girl, then, what's she called again?

MAUD: Dora (Beetle they call her). She left before I started here – she's busy out in Syria with her family, of all places! She has three little ones and the youngest is a little boy called Roger. She's out there, looking after all those refugees, and with that baby, I don't know how she manages. I know her mother worries about her living over there in all that heat. Can you imagine? Her husband Ernest was injured in the Great War, but he bounced back. They are both working now, in the hospital, bless 'em.

ALBERT: Blimey … what a family!

MAUD: Ay …! What a family.

Sharing

The group were very excited to be invited to attend and exhibit their work at the Collingwood Conference and Exhibition in Cardiff University at the Arts and Social Science Library in April 2018. The group interacted with the attendees which included members of the family, artists, historians and archivists, demonstrating their artwork but also giving two presentations, one including Maud's chat with Albert and the other which included the evaluations and asked the attendees what wellbeing was to them. The group were particularly delighted to be invited to have their work added to the archive after it had been on display with the exhibition of the Collingwood archive. Edith was speaking to them: "In every child an artist".

It was immensely rewarding to be part of the group, surrounded by such inspiring material and to have the opportunity to work together to create the miniature books.

'Through the Trees' Rookwood project

Following on from the Collingwood Project Louise spent some time working on applying for a new project and made the error of planning something

Figure 6.10 Archived Collingwood creations.

much bigger than she had capacity for. After all, she had a part-time job, a family and home to look after and an elderly mother to attend to. So, she dropped all thoughts of doing a project at all and let her mind take a break from it all. It was not long after this, however, that she could feel those tell-tale signs of curiosity nudging at her. What was it that Simone Joslyn (Head of the Cardiff and Vale Health Charity) had said about Rookwood Hospital? An old Victorian house, with some archives. What were these archives? What history lay within those walls? What could we learn from these people and the place they lived in?

Box 6.2 Short history of Rookwood

Rookwood was first built in 1886 by Sir Edward Hill, a South Wales businessman who transported coal around the world. At this time the mansion was built as a family residence.

In 1918 the Rookwood Mansion was taken over by the Red Cross and used as a convalescent home for soldiers returning from the Great War.

At the end of the First World War it was purchased by Sir Lawrence Phillips who presented it to the Ministry as a home for Welsh Paraplegic Pensioners. It was subsequently used by the University Hospital of Wales and then in 1932 it became a General Hospital where, once again during the Second World War, it was used for injured service personnel.

During the 1970s and 80s, Rookwood had eight wards caring for people with spinal injuries, brain injury, stroke, multiple sclerosis and Parkinson's disease. Rookwood Hospital has for many years been a long-term rehabilitation hospital, and a specialist centre dealing in artificial limbs and appliances. It is set within beautiful grounds, first planted and developed by the Hill family, and boasting, it is said, a selection of trees from every part of the world,

The building itself, however, is sadly now no longer fit for purpose, and the staff and patients are soon to be relocated to University Hospital Llandough.

Eventually, Louise met with Simone and when visiting the hospital with her, and more specifically the old wood panelled boardroom with its calm interior and huge long stately table, she was firmly hooked. It was clear that the gardens, and the trees therein, held an important place for the Hill family, and for the many people who had since lived and worked there. The sense of peace within the grounds of Rookwood clearly contributed an enormous amount to the environment in which so many people had spent their time, in healing and rehabilitating. This legacy of trees, then, was the thing that she

Figure 6.11 View of Rookwood boardroom.

was drawn to most, and shortly after their meeting, the 'Through the Trees' project was conceived of, to be funded by the Cardiff and Vale Health Charity, and subsequently planned for the spring of 2018.

She would be running an initial session in the Glamorgan Archives in which a group would be exploring some old scrapbooks, put together by the Hill family. This would be followed by three arts workshops which would take place in the hospital itself, exploring the gardens and taking any findings back to the boardroom where they would explore a number of different monoprint techniques. For this project, as for the Collingwood, Louise would be the creative lead for the workshops.

The participants

Former participants in the Stiwdio Arts Group projects were invited to take part in the project along with NHS staff members. The workshops were planned in such a way that staff could attend in shorter standalone sessions, as their time, in many cases, was limited. Although staff showed interest in the project, none of them came along and so with a view to extending the participation in the project, Louise later held a couple of extra sessions involving patients from two wards and the occupational therapy staff who supported them.

Altogether there were thirteen participants in the project, including the artist, Marion Cheung, who was concurrently running another arts project in Rookwood Hospital and Rachel Lewis, one of the hospital chaplains who very kindly invited Louise into Rookwood Chapel as a space to meet and think. As well as being involved as participants, their input was very welcome, offering as they did both support and feedback.

Research and design

Louise spent some time over the winter period researching the Hill family and working on some print techniques that she was particularly keen to share with the group. Her aim was to introduce techniques that were relatively simple, but also challenging. She wanted to offer the chance to learn something new whilst also producing something that each person could be pleased with.

Both strands of work, the archival investigations and the print techniques, could be absorbing and generative, but for Louise the most exciting part of the project was the research into the trees. She was identifying the different species, conceiving a trail of specific trees that could be followed around the landscaped grounds, and chatting with the gardeners and other staff within the hospital. They offered their response to the trees, and shared lots of information. By creating the trail of trees and furnishing each 'station' with information, both about the trees themselves and about some of the Rookwood stories, she would be able to share these with the group and with other subsequent visitors to Rookwood. Any art work produced by the group would be the product of their time spent in this environment, sharing the space together and taking the time to walk around the garden, to look at the trees and respond to what could be seen and collected along the way.

The plan was to run a number of day-long workshops in the old boardroom and then to finish the project in mid-June with a guided tour of the trail of trees and an exhibition of the work produced.

Delivery

Louise began researching and designing the 'Through the Trees' project in November 2018 and found herself visiting Rookwood in deepest winter! Some of the work she produced reflects that rather dour period. As the spring drew nearer, however, she was inspired by the notion of creating a trail that patients and visitors alike would be able to follow around the grounds of Rookwood, identifying certain trees along the way, whatever the weather.

The final handout notes for the 'Trail of Trees' included pictures of these trees, taken or drawn on different occasions over a six-month period.

Day one

For our first workshop we visited the Glamorgan Archives and researched a little of the history of Rookwood by delving into the eleven Hill family scrapbooks that are kept on their shelves. We were also helped in our quest by Gwawr Falconbridge from the Whitchurch Historical Society who kindly passed on many other documents relating to the local history. Our findings were gathered together into the 'Historical Dossier', a large black file, which, when needed in the course of the project, we were able to refer to.

Day two

The second workshop took place a month later and this time we were in the hospital itself. We began by wending our way around the grounds, along the trail of trees, not only focusing on the trees themselves, but also on the shapes that were created around them, the spaces in between. The inspiration for the first set of collagraphs came from the magnolia tree and the cherry blossoms, and the beautiful negative spaces created in between their branches.

Box 6.3a The sycamore

The wood from the sycamore has been traditionally used to make violins. It inspires music and dance and is a symbol of the creative arts.

Rookwood is home to many sycamores and it has always been a place where music and song have played a large part. In the days when the Hill family lived here, garden parties and concerts were held regularly.

Box 6.3b The Wellingtonia

These trees, named after the Duke of Wellington, stand majestic and imposing in stature with an eerie symmetry. The two trees were planted by Sir Edward Stock Hill in honour of his two sons. They bear witness to the changing of the times and seasons over the last 150 years as people have come and gone and the place has provided different purposes.

Figure 6.12 Wellingtonia tree.

We spent the rest of the morning creating a collagraph plate each, which we would be able to print from later. Whilst waiting for the plate to dry Louise introduced the group to the watercolour monoprints that she had been experimenting with. Using leaves from the garden we placed them in varying positions on paper, doused them in watery watercolour paint and weighed them down with rocks and stones. These were then put away for the following week when we would be able to see the fully dried results. This technique can produce some beautiful results in quite an unpredictable and delightful way.

Box 6.3c The cherry blossom (Mayflower)

The cherry blossom tree, or mayflower, as it is known by some, originates mainly from Japan where it is revered and celebrated with ceremonial receptions called Hanami in the early spring.

These trees and their flowering symbolise an omen of good fortune, an emblem of love and affection, and an enduring metaphor for the fleeting nature of mortality. They mark the arrival of new beginnings and are famous for the beautiful festoons of blossom, bringing with them a sense of enthusiasm and optimism for things to come. The inspiration for some of the work in the 'Through the Trees' project came from the magnolia tree and the cherry blossoms, and the beautiful negative spaces created in between their branches.

Box 6.3d The magnolia

Just in front of the old Rookwood Mansion House sits the beautiful magnolia tree which both staff and patients alike have a great fondness for. Although the blossoming time is sadly short-lived, it comes early in the spring, and is a welcome sight after the dark days of winter. Behind it, in the old Rookwood Mansion, are the rooms which see the running of the hospital in all its aspects, and the beautiful chapel whose doors are always open for anyone wishing to visit.

Day three

On the morning of the third workshop we retrieved our watercolour monoprints and revealed the results to one another. There was a wonderful delicacy in much of the work and each person had chosen their own combination of colours. We shared each other's work with curiosity and pleasure.

Box 6.3e The tulip tree

The tulip tree is a member of the magnolia family and only starts to flower when it is over 20 years old. Fossilised samples of this tree date back to 95 million years ago.

Perhaps it was the allure of this tree that drew so many bees to make their home in the Elderly Care and Assessment Unit which overlooks the gardens. In August 2016 honey was reported to have been dripping down the walls of this unit and on investigation a huge beehive was found in the ceiling. The warmth from the hot summer sun had melted the wax and enabled the honey to seep out and down the walls. About 110,000 bees were subsequently removed from the roof and were given a new home in Lancashire.

The rest of the morning was spent on a new technique of creating a leaf relief with leaves, foil and cardboard. These, along with our first collagraph plates, were subsequently used to print from, experimenting both with colour and with the transparency and opacity of the inks. There was an air of busyness in the room as people concentrated on achieving a print or two, finishing their plates and surveying their work to date.

The session ended with a brief word from Louise about the following workshops which would resume after the Easter holidays.

Figure 6.13 Tulip tree.

Box 6.3f The oak tree

In the grounds of Rookwood there is an enormous oak, planted over 100 years ago and standing amongst the melee of trees in the woodland area of the grounds. In Britain the oak tree is associated with longevity; it is a symbol of power, of strength and survival and it has always played an important part in culture. In the 1500s couples were married under ancient oaks and in the festive season, the yule logs were traditionally cut from oak trees. It is host to more life than any other British tree and in folklore it is a symbol of warm, deep love, its boughs and roots large enough to hold all the joy and pain of life.

Box 6.3g The monkey puzzle tree

This was one of the trees that Sir Edward Hill planted during his time in Rookwood. Because of the longevity of this species, it is described as a living fossil and is also the national tree of Chile, so named because it was believed that no monkey would be able to climb it.

Originally there were two monkey puzzle trees in the grounds, but sadly, Rookwood lost the first one, much to the dismay of staff and patients, when one day completely out of the blue it just toppled over and fell into the car park!

The second one remains, strong and proud, standing tall in front of the Old Summerhouse, which is now hidden behind a mesh of trees. The summerhouse dates back to the thirteenth century and was resurrected in Rookwood for the Hill family.

Day four and five

The last session was to be run over two days to allow time for finishing off. The intention had been to create an artist's book together, perhaps featuring throughout its pages the themes that had been touched on as the project had unfolded. We had seen the old summer house in the garden, hidden by a tangle of trees and branches, and Jane had produced a beautiful poem in response to it and shared it with the group (see Box 7.4). We had talked about the sense of the past in the present, the whispers of the past as contained in some of the more ephemeral qualities of the work. We had talked about psithurism (see Box 7.2), the sound of the wind, as mediated through the trees; about the way the gardens had been a place of joy, celebration and music, hosting parties and fetes in summers spanning over 150 years. We had been bowled over by the enormity of the two Wellingtonia trees (see Box 6.3b), standing testament and memorial to past lives and contributing endlessly to the sense of calm, healing and balm within that lovingly landscaped garden.

Box 6.3h The mulberry tree

There are only a few mulberry trees in Cardiff, and this is one of them. It sits here, quite unassuming, and to a certain extent unnoticed.

Mulberry trees were originally brought to Britain by the Romans who used the leaves to treat diseases of the mouth and lungs, whilst in the 1600s the bark of their roots was used to expel tapeworm from the gut. Now they are known for their fruit, the long dark red berries which grow in the summer. The staff described the juice from these berries as a strikingly brilliant, deep, staining blood red. The fruit is considered to have many healing properties, helping to lower cholesterol, improve blood circulation, improve digestive health, reduce cancer risk, cure anaemia, and the list goes on.

We had explored the idea of the spaces in between, and of those 'spaces' as also being those precious moments in between, spent in time out, taken in between the stresses and strains of everyday life.

To allow for the variety of responses to our days spent in Rookwood, it was decided that we would make individual collages, and these, it was hoped, would be a more robust presentation if the hospital wished to display them on their walls. We each had a box frame, about an inch deep, allowing space for the layering of materials, paper and objects. We were invited to use anything from the things we had already made, whether it was the watercolours, or the collagraphs, or the leaf prints to create a piece that might in some way reflect the things that we had been exploring. In addition, anything could be sought from the raggedy-bag collection of old materials and the bits and pieces that Louise and Rachel had brought in.

Once these were finished, we gave our pieces a title, all of which had their own resonances:

Light and Life Through The trees
Night Blooms
Green Pyjamas
Skylight
A Broken Thing
Hessian Nights
A Winter's Spring
Not Forgotten

Sharing

Over forty people attended the guided walk and exhibition on the midsummer morning in June. It was a gentle affair and the stroll around the grounds was an enjoyable one with the rain holding off for the duration.

Box 6.4 Advert for tree trail exhibition

Join us in discovering

The Rookwood Trail – A Treasury of Trees

Anyone who has ever visited, stayed or worked in Rookwood Hospital cannot help but have noticed the wonderful trees that grow so abundantly in the grounds. Sir Edward Stock Hill was the original owner of Rookwood in the mid-1800s.

This spring a group of artists, volunteers and NHS staff members took part in the 'Through the Trees' Arts for Wellbeing project, and were given the opportunity to work in the atmospheric Rookwood boardroom. Over these few months the 'Rookwood Trail' began to emerge and the group were able to create some pieces of work in response to this and to the beautiful and historic setting they found themselves in.

You are invited to join us as we take a guided tour along the 'Rookwood Trail', following its path around the old mansion house and identifying some of the remarkable trees along the way.

11.20 am – Assemble in Rookwood Chapel
11.30 am – A guided walk along the Rookwood Trail
12.15 pm – Refreshments in the Chapel, and Exhibition

As we follow the trail, we will touch on some of the local history of Rookwood, from Victorian times to the present day, and reflect on how trees can so often hold special meaning for us.

The walk will be followed by refreshments in the chapel and an opportunity to see some of the artwork to come out of the 'Through the Trees' project.

All welcome

Summary

This chapter has described the development and projects of the Stiwdio Arts Group. They were developed with some understanding of the evidence base but also using an experimental but phenomenological approach. Each project started with a pilot to check structure, media and resources. The projects were then created within a local context in time and place. There can be found essential elements to the projects and their outcomes, but each project has its unique place and time; the phenomenon cannot be precisely reproduced but the lived experiences within the participants, leaders and members of the public can be learnt from in the promotion of wellbeing.

All the project received evaluations that included the following:

- More satisfied with life, more happiness
- Creations
- Opportunity to learn
- Company of others
- Time to focus

In addition, the individual variations included:

- Words and images
- The bee project
- Portraits

'Artist in the Making' Collingwood project

- Time to engage with warmth and comfort
- Freedom

'Through the Trees' Rookwood project

- Love, care and hope
- Time for silence and laughter
- Engaging, intriguing, magical and relaxing

Chapter 7

Evaluations, reflections and creations

Introduction

This chapter offers responses from the participants to the Artists in the Making and Through the Trees projects undertaken by the Stiwdio Arts Group as described in Chapter 6. It includes the written evaluations taken at the end of the projects, participant reflections and some of their creations.

The Artists in the Making project's evaluations were compared to the Department of Health (HM Gov. 2010) definition of wellbeing, Diener and Suh's (1997) measures of wellbeing and Ryff's (1989) psychological well-being. All of these, despite their age, are used as foundational texts in the area of wellbeing. After this first attempt to quantify the evaluations to offer a robust justification for further funding it was decided to change to a more qualitative approach as the measures available were inadequate to capture the rich tapestry of the experiences being explored. This can easily be seen within the text.

To explore whether the projects were improving the participants' mental wellbeing it was still necessary to identify the phenomenon being explored. Mental wellbeing was identified as a subjective experience that can, at times, be measured objectively. Therefore, it was important to also explore self before making assumptions about impact on mental wellbeing. Wellbeing was explored in Chapter 2, self in Chapter 3, history, temporality and culture in Chapter 4 and Chapter 5 explored creativity. These explorations led to the following terms of reference.

Mental wellbeing

In Chapter 2 an examination of philosophy, anthropology and psychology led to establishing that the *key to understanding wellbeing is through the experience of joy mediated by the body, truth, beauty and/or the divine, which makes suffering in life experiences meaningful and worthwhile.*

Self

Self was explored in Chapter 3 and many scientific terms were identified but the definition in keeping with a psychological phenomenological approach and the one accepted here is: Self: *the interaction between an individual's 'felt sense' which provides meaning through embodied relational knowing and the world in which the person lives in time and space.*

History, temporality and culture

Chapter 4 took a journey through the importance of history for self-concept and wellbeing including an understanding of time and its place in culture. This was necessary as ancestry and history were both found to be of intrinsic and extrinsic value in the projects. No clear definition of ancestry and history in this context was uncovered as the evidence base for a link between history and wellbeing is limited by methodological issues. The evidence available does indicate that involvement in history supports subjective experiences of wellbeing. Philosophers such as Gendlin, Todres, Tilley and Malpas (see Chapter 4) all identify that there is more to an experience than can be summed up by what can be seen and measured. The rich tapestry of life can only be appreciated by embodied interaction with the world and each other including a recognition that experiences occur in time and space.

Creativity

Chapter 5 states that the evidence indicates creative activities can have a healing and protective effect on mental wellbeing but there are limitations to the current evidence base.

Creativity is a complex phenomenon to define, leading to Plucker *et al.* (2004: 86) stating it is a "fuzzy, soft construct" which promotes mythologising, unfounded definitions and confusion. To some extent this has led to different explanations of creativity depending on where and how it is being used. The three types of creativity in relation to wellbeing are:

- Structural – a personality trait
- Cognitive process – an ability everyone can achieve
- Sociocultural – interactional and contextual

These three approaches to understanding creativity also offer an approach to understanding mental wellbeing:

- Structural – a personal trait such as resilience
- Cognitive process – managing emotion and restructuring thoughts
- Sociocultural – influenced by others and the environment

Table 7.1 Evaluation statements related to theories of wellbeing using the Department of Health (2007), Diener and Suh (1997) and Ryff (1989)

Department of Health		*Diener and Suh*		*Ryff*	
Healthy	Not mentioned	Life satisfaction	All statements	Autonomy	The chance to experiment Access to the collection
Happy	Freedom to do our art as part of project The chance to experiment The company of other members Access to the collection Being influential to others potentially Having something nice that I had made at the end of the project and seeing other people do the same	Pleasant affect	Freedom to do our art as part of project The chance to experiment The company of other members Being influential to others potentially Having something nice that I had made at the end of the project and seeing other people do the same Enjoyable; felt like I could make and finish something Time to focus on positive, warm and comforting about people and history, which makes me feel warmer and more comfortable	Environmental mastery	Freedom to do our art as part of project Learning about watercolours, drawing with ink and more about this family The company of other members Being influential to others potentially Having something nice that I had made at the end of the project and seeing other people do the same Enjoyable; felt like I could make and finish something
Contented	The company of other members Having something nice that I had made at the end of the project and seeing other people do the same	Unpleasant affect	None identified	Positive relationships with others	The company of other members Having something nice that I had made, at the end of the project and seeing other people do the same Being part of the group and enjoying the activity

Comfort	The chance to experiment The company of other members Time to focus on positive, warm and comforting about people and history, which makes me feel warmer and more comfortable		Purpose in life	Freedom to do our art as part of projectHaving something nice that I had made at the end of the project and seeing other people do the same
Satisfied	All statements		Realisation of potential	The chance to experiment Learning about watercolours, drawing with ink and more about this family Being influential to others potentially Having something nice that I had made at the end of the project and seeing other people do the same Enjoyable, felt like I could make and finish something

continued

Table 7.1 continued

Department of Health	*Diener and Suh*	*Ryff*	
		Self-acceptance	Access to the collection Being influential to others potentially Having something nice that I had made at the end of the project and seeing other people do the same Enjoyable, felt like I could make and finish something Time to focus on positive, warm and comforting about people and history, which makes me feel warmer and more comfortable

Table 7.2 Evaluation statements compared to Department of Health (2007) dimensions of wellbeing

Department of Health dimensions of wellbeing	*Participants' statements*
Physical	*Not mentioned*
Material	*Having something nice that I had made at the end of the project and seeing other people do the same* *To be able to view the tiny beautiful pictures and to gain awareness of how it was to live in the nineteenth century*
Social	*Seeing the personal possessions and artworks from a whole family, very interesting to see them all in relation to each other* *Being part of the group and enjoying the activity* *Getting in touch and socialising*
Emotional	*To be able to view the tiny beautiful pictures and to gain awareness of how it was to live in the nineteenth century* *Enjoyable, felt like I could make and finish something* *Being part of the group and enjoying the activity* *Time to focus on positive, warm and comforting about people and history, which makes me feel warmer and more comfortable*
Developmental	*Interest in archives, the author's family, and how this could relate to doing work* *Sounded interesting* *Learning new areas and art, history and meeting people* *Learning new techniques, the company of other members, opportunity to undertake an artistic activity*
Activity	*To do something creative, something new* *Getting to see and touch the objects/books* *Being part of the group and enjoying the activity* *Learning new techniques, the company of other members, opportunity to undertake an artistic activity*

For this book, through using a phenomenological lifeworld approach all these features are acknowledged as playing a role in mental wellbeing. As this chapter is read it is important to recognise each element only offers one lens, one small keyhole through which to understand how the projects affected the participants' mental wellbeing.

Artist in the making reflection: Louise

When I was first invited to come along with the Stiwdio Arts project to explore the Collingwood Collection I was of course very pleased, but also, when seeing what a large and manifold collection it was, a little overwhelmed. The family spanned over three or four generations and the family tree was like a large oak with many branches.

I knew that in order to tap into the wealth of this extraordinary family, the important thing to do would be to choose one moment when this part of the family would be in focus, a prism through which we could see the refracted light that shone through them.

As I was being introduced to the material I was particularly drawn to the sketchbooks of the Collingwood family with William and Edith at their head circa the mid-1880s. In particular there were some beautiful pages in which Edith had taken each of the children's drawings, over a number of years, and kept a record of what they had done, from as young as four and upwards, noting down, I assume for their benefit, as well as for her own, the small developments she could see in their work pointing to what they needed to work on further. These documents were a wonderful window into the whole culture of their family life and creative work. If looking at this collection was to yield anything up to me it would be a strong sense of Edith as both mother and teacher. If she were to speak to me today, I believe that one of the things she would say to me would be that in every child there is an artist.

The first time we all met at the library where the archives were stored was a really odd experience. We all stood round a large table with the archives laid out and it was as if we were revering it; we all appeared in awe and respectful of what was laid out in front of us. I was immediately drawn to the tiny pictures of animals drawn by the children. In a way I wanted to get to know them but it was more than that, it was a more visceral experience.

I found the whole experience moving; I was anxious about what the others would think of my artwork and I thought they would all have high expectations of me but no one was critical of anyone. Everyone found positive things to say about everything. The group made me feel safe, secure and comfortable.

The exercise 'What Maud Thought' produced a distillation of what the group had come to know about the family members and was an opportunity to add another dimension to our thinking of the Collingwoods. We had become increasingly aware as the project went on that they were a privileged family, of a very particular class, and it was a chance to add to this mix. It was

Figure 7.1 Picture of Maud.

a quick-fire rendering of Maud's view of the family members, and yet stands as testament to much of what we had learnt over the three days, her words sitting happily beside our pictures of the lake. the miniature books, our splodgy watercolours and beautiful play with ink.

The 'What Maud Thought' exercise was really interesting. We all shared on pieces of paper in short sentences what we thought Maud would think of each of the Collingwoods and amazingly we developed quite rounded personalities. Through the artwork they had produced and some of their letters we had all come to see this family as real people that we could jointly recognise. We felt we had a relationship with them.

We had worked on the Collingwoods, peeked into their lives, drawn out our perceptions of them and their work, and begun to understand them as children, as the people they became, and as the artists they were, in the making. As a group we had gone on a journey of sorts, and we had been creating and working together towards our portrait of this family, and in doing so, also positioning ourselves as artists in the making.

From the outset, Judith, as the project archivist, played a significant role in our exploration. I was struck from the very first time she spoke to me about the family. To her, each of them was a fully rounded person. She called them by their first names; she had spent hours already working through their letters, diaries, notes and annotations, getting to know them, both from their own writings and drawings, as well as from the way they wrote to each other, and referred to each other. Judith was, throughout the project, a rich source of information for us, not least because she carried with her a sense of this family as being very real, present, and human, with all of their own foibles, talents and concerns.

It was lovely to see the journeys of each of the Collingwood children, and in doing so, it certainly encouraged me to look at my own journey as an artist, and my own role as a mother and a facilitator of other people's work. Keep at it, keep practically doing, work at the problems, see it as a work in progress, and give the work the status it deserves, whatever stage it is at.

It was also immensely rewarding to be part of the group, surrounded by such inspiring material and to have the opportunity to work together to create the miniature books. These are being exhibited tonight, and the group are really happy to have been asked if they can be accepted into the archive, with Edith speaking to us: 'In every child an artist'.

After the Collingwood project I attended and contributed to a conference hosted by Cardiff University about the Collingwood collection, and had the opportunity to hear some archivists talking about their work.

I was very struck by one observation that as an archivist one gets drawn ultimately to what interests you and what sparks your curiosity. That was certainly my experience when I first encountered the Collingwood collection; I was drawn very specifically to Edith Collingwood, and her role as a home-school teacher. I was drawn to the children and the work they had produced as children, and I was curious to know how they had turned out, and if there was a connection with this way of teaching them in their early years.

In particular, I was drawn to how she had been with her children, as a mother, as an artist and as an educator. She had annotated their work carefully and kept all of their work in chronological order, noting how they were developing along the way. To me, this was in some ways astounding, and it is for two reasons. First, because she was giving so much status to the notion and practice of working artistically, and second she was giving status to each of the children individually, really reflecting back to them, with a degree of gravity, their agency in the world. What they did, what they had produced, mattered.

Calling the project 'The Collingwood children – Artists in the making' I had chosen to focus on this moment in the Collingwood family history.

Even though I had chosen a somewhat slender window, the material on offer to the group was so rich that it had the scope to offer everybody something. By choosing one of the family to focus on and to create a portrait of them, we would be spending lots of time quietly absorbing and exploring the things that attracted us about that particular person.

It was only by the end of the project that I realised what a personal journey I had been involved in, focusing on these young children and the encouragement of their mother.

Reflecting on my own bouts of depression, I know that when I disintegrate into them it is with a tortured lack of self-esteem. I feel of no consequence, can see no value to what I am or what I do. There is a blindly subjective feeling of spiralling inwards, painfully spiralling down into a state of non-existence.

Whether or not I can work creatively is somewhere completely bound up in this sense of worthlessness. The creation of the Stiwdio Arts Group, and the decision to work creatively in this forum, was itself a push back in the other direction, to square up to this feeling and work against it. This push back is a practical, searching, curious drive that reaches out to speak to other people and asks to be seen, however modestly, and asks to be of some agency in the world.

So to spend time exploring the sketchbooks of a family who valued each and every child to work in this way was an enormous encouragement to me, supporting the drive in me to continue.

It also, importantly, told me that being an artist is a process, that it is about those practical questions, all the time tangling with one's own abilities, reaching that bit further every time and exploring the materials that we use anew. It's about not taking the unsuccessful moments as failures, but about being ready to pick up and start again having learnt the lessons.

Box 7.1a Conference: what is wellbeing? April 2018

These are the words written on bunting by members of the conference in response to a presentation of the project, but some people provided small drawings instead. The presentation considered what wellbeing might mean and the impact the project might and did have on the participants.

Wellbeing is:

- Work and life balance
- Calm
- *Benessere, bien-être, wohlsein*
- Family, nature, books!
- A shared purpose filled existence
- Sleep, family, outdoors, reading, friends
- Engaging with music
- Sense of achievement!
- Buy a skateboard
- Comfortable
- Boat
- Surrounding yourself with people who make you happy
- A day without pain or exhaustion and tiredness
- My garden, my dog, my family and friends, my work, cooking
- Solving self-set challenge, having someone to share with, a newborn grandson, a good journey, a cuddly toy to chat with, listening to Beethoven's violin concerto on a summer's day

- Laughing enough, sharing humorous attitude
- Purposeful, energetic, engagement (the chance or ability to do so)
- Relaxed, well fed, listening to 'Walter's Prize Song' at the end of Die Meistersinger with a glass of a good red wine in my hand
- A day walking in the hills in pleasant company

Box 7.1b Distilled understanding of wellbeing

Whilst the individual items identified such as 'a skateboard' are idiosyncratic, most of the elements of wellbeing identified here are the same as those identified in the available literature.

Table 7.3 Conference wellbeing statements compared to categories of wellbeing

Fun	Buy a skateboard	Laughing enough, sharing humorous attitude		
Engagement with pleasurable activity	Nature, books! Boat, outdoors, reading	Solving self-set challenge, having someone to share with, a newborn grandson, a good journey, a cuddly toy to chat with, listening to Beethoven's violin concerto on a summer's day	Engaging with music, energetic, engagement (the chance or ability to do so) listening to Walter's 'Prize Song' at the end of Die Meistersinger with a glass of a good red wine in my hand	My garden, my dog, my family & friends, my work, cooking, a day walking in the hills in pleasant company.
Calm/rest/ comfort	Calm	Sleep, family, outdoors, reading, friends	Comfortable	Relaxed, well-fed, listening to Walter's 'Prize Song' at the end of Die Meistersinger with a glass of a good red wine in my hand
Balance	Work and life balance			
All languages/ cultures	*Benessere, bien-être, wohlsein*			

Relationships/ others	Family, my dog, my family & friends	A shared purpose-filled existence, laughing enough, sharing humorous attitude	Surrounding yourself with people who make you happy	Having someone to share with, a day walking in the hills in pleasant company
Purpose	A shared purpose-filled existence	Sense of achievement!	Purposeful, energetic engagement (the chance or ability to do so)	
Physical	A day without pain or exhaustion and tiredness			

Artist in the making reflection: Daisy

The first day of the project we met at a café and I was late; I hate being late and I felt embarrassed when I was asked what I wanted to drink so I asked for water. I only knew Louise a little and I did not know the others at all. I thought they would all have high expectations of me because I worked at the university, so I tried not to tell them. I was anxious about how I looked, the clothes I was wearing, and extremely concerned that I might say something that might offend someone. I kept trying to appear calm and confident, but I just wanted to run away. When Judith the archivist arrived, we all walked to the university archives. Louise's elderly mother was with us, she immediately made me feel strong, caring and capable. She gave me the perfect excuse to walk slowly with her, talking to her and appearing to look after her. I think she was really caring for me!

When we got into the library special editions archive, I felt a bit awestruck, the room was bright and light; it felt air conditioned. There were lots of pieces on display, lots of pictures, post cards and pieces of writing. Judith told us a bit about the archive and the family then we were allowed to look through what had been set out for us, she said she would photocopy anything we wanted to work with. I was afraid to touch anything in case I damaged it, but Judith supported us in our viewing of the material. I loved the tiny pictures of animals drawn by the children and felt rather drawn to Ursula the youngest daughter. She seemed to be her own person and the least artistic. I do not consider myself artistic at all, but I love drawing and painting and doing needlework.

By the end of the first day I comfortable with Judith, Louise and Louise's mother but I still felt unsure about the rest of the group despite no one doing anything to upset me.

The second day I was again late, I got lost on the way and so was nearly in tears when I arrived but Louise encouraged me to get a hot drink and then when everyone else was busy spent some time at my side explaining what they were doing. We were using photocopies of the pictures we had identified and transferring them onto linen. It was a simple task but with really good effects and we used these pictures as the front of our little accordion style booklets. The others in the group had quite mixed abilities; some were really artistic in their development of their booklets and others were idealistic and so overdid bits, but I was very pleased with my success and strangely I didn't need everyone to say how good it was.

I had had a successful day, despite being late and everyone had treated me as if I was normal and did not seem to have any particular expectations of me. I happily did not get lost going home.

Day 3 late again! I got even more lost this time than last time; everywhere looked the same so I could not tell which street to go down. I was having a bad week before getting to the project – I had been assaulted a few days before and been left feeling guilty, bruised and very sorry for myself. When I arrived, everyone smiled at me and showed concern about my getting lost again. I tried to respond by laughing at myself, but it was difficult. Louise seemed to understand and gave me some space.

Figure 7.2 Accordion booklets.

I don't know if anyone else noticed but at lunchtime one of the guys started telling me he was not feeling so well today. We stood outside looking at the gardens and he told me how he was struggling with his energy and his ability to think. I know it sounds unkind but it sort of made me feel better; being able to listen to someone else and them wanting to talk to me about something sensitive.

In the afternoon we continued to work on our miniature booklets, and it was wonderful to be able to focus on something pretty. I liked to think about Ursula being encouraged by her mother to draw and paint sitting in pretty Edwardian clothes in the sunshine overlooking the lake. It was as if I was taking on some of her experiences; I started to feel more feminine and pretty. I felt as if instead of being in that small cold art room I was there by the lake with her, a loving and encouraging mother, warm sunshine, feeling confident and happy.

I loved doing the artwork but the most amusing thing we did was develop Maud's conversation with her brother. We each wrote down individually what we thought she would say about the different members of the family and were surprised with how detailed but similar our views were. The funniest thing was when Louise read out what Maud would say in a Northern accent. Louise was brilliant at being Maud and we all laughed!

'Through the Trees' project reflection: Louise

Coming to Rookwood was something rather different. I was drawn to the trees, to their silence, to their solidity, and in the first instance during those winter months, their silhouetted beauty against the sky. I have been very aware, as has everyone I know, of the social and political context in which the project took place and particularly here in Britain where there has been a sense of a prolonged and painful transition, a not knowing, a lack of solution or of resolution. When the project began in March, the augured exit of Britain from the European Union was still not materialising, leaving the country holding polarised views and no easy way forward.

It was during this time that I saw a television programme about Japanese gardens with Monty Don. At one point he was in a landscaped public park talking to an elderly Japanese man about the way in which the branches of the trees were held up with poles as they grew, to keep them supported, how the shapes of the branches and taking the journey from one tree to the next was as important as seeing the trees when they are in leaf, or in blossom. He talked about the Japanese concept of *ma*, of the negative space in between the trees and the importance of this space. Lastly, he talked about how walking through the trees, winding one's way along the trail, can change one's sense of being, becoming a little more aware and perhaps calmer.

On further investigation I discovered that the concept of *ma* extended to something a little more again.

> The Japanese idea of *ma* is that we need to create interruptions or absences that allow for difference to be reconciled. Designing for *ma* is about creating moments of awareness and quiet.... Cities are scattered with small parks that appear suddenly and offer winding trails for quiet reflection. Even conversations in Japanese are marked by long pauses that would be unsettling for Western ears.... Being intentional about creating spaces that allow for reflection and integration might allow us to better address some of the contradictions and tensions of modern life.
>
> (McGrath 2018)

I was immediately taken with this notion, as it seems to speak so eloquently both to the situation we are in and to some ways in which we can mitigate against its effects.

Keen to share it with the group, I planned the first session as a walk in the grounds, with me relaying these ideas about *ma* and us standing in front of the cherry blossom and magnolia trees, looking at the branches of both of these trees and noting their beautiful line against the sky. They were to be our first models for the workshop. The idea of *ma* stayed with us, and throughout the weeks of the project became a frame of reference for the group, where we spoke about the need to have a little *ma* time, and a recognition that this space in which we gathered and the time that we had together offered us just this thing.

The Trail of Trees fitted in perfectly with the notion of spaces that allow for reflection and integration. 'Rookwood – Through the Trees' was very much a project about resilience in times of stress and transition.

'Through the Trees' project reflection: Monica

> The process was surprising with elements of chance ever-present. Engaging, intriguing, magical and relaxing!

I am a freelance artist and workshop leader working with diverse groups in diverse settings – in addition to commercial work, I lead creative art sessions with patients and staff at a hospital and work with primary schools and community groups.

When I heard that artist Louise Jensen would be running a series of experimental print workshops in the same location that I would be delivering my workshops, I looked forward to meeting and finding out more about her project. I could even take up her offer of joining the activities of the group.

It provided an opportunity to collaborate and investigate any similarities there might be.

Prior to this, I had been suffering a creative block concerning my own personal work. I had just completed an intense project and had been ill over

Christmas and New Year. As an artist and teacher I spend a lot of time planning activities. It involves much attention to detail – planning for the unexpected. I mustn't forget to bring anything to a workshop. The pressure is always on, including the pressure to find work and new projects to pay the bills.

I am not alone or unusual in the amount of planning that I put into a workshop that only lasts one or two hours. For every hour of delivery, two hours of planning can go into it. I am not alone as an artist striving for the best experiences for participants – after all, a good experience depends on if I get invited back to work again and is a constant pressure. I tend to doubt my abilities when I know I shouldn't. This level of anxiety and stress is ever-present no matter what kind of work I do. Other people might say, "You care too much …" but I can't help it. I am not alone in giving my all and occasionally my ideas away to other people so that they can get out of a rut themselves. As Julia Cameron explains in her book *The Artist's Way*, this behaviour can lead to over-mining the 'artistic well' leading to creative burnout, so artists beware.

How then, as an artist juggling many demands (the usual work/life/family balance) do you find that much needed space in order to recuperate and be yourself and not a million and one things to other people?

When I started the workshops, I didn't realise just how important taking part would be and how it would make me feel … what it would be like to experience being on 'the other side' receiving guidance on printmaking techniques. How would it make me feel to leave my ego outside (after all I came from a printmaking background and should know a lot about this) and wipe the slate clean to try something new?

One of the processes produced sophisticated results, yet it was surprisingly simple to achieve … all it needed was space and a bit of time. Could I make something as beautiful as that?

I'd never met the group before and had only met the creative lead on two occasions. Workshops would take place in the boardroom – a huge, darkly gothic room on the ground floor of Rookwood Hospital – a place steeped in history. At one end, large double doors opened out onto the gardens – we were so close to nature and could see the rooks, trees rustling in the wind and hear birdsong. Welcomed with tea and biscuits (never underestimate the power of a cuppa), the group was friendly and diverse.

Hidden illnesses and a chance encounter had brought us together. Anxiety, depression, phobias, creative blocks … how could taking part do anything to shift these feelings and put us on a different path?

Louise introduced the project in a friendly, unassuming yet knowledgeable way. She had meticulously laid the room out. Absolutely everything we could possibly need was there and within easy reach. It must have taken ages to prepare. We went outside for a walk in the hospital grounds. Not for the sake of it, we looked up at trees, in between branches and not down at our phones. We made conversations that weren't about why we were here or what had happened. Instead, we were introduced to the Japanese concept of *ma* – the spaces between things. Spaces in between branches, leaves and the air. Spaces to rest. Spaces in between busy-ness and nothing. Spaces to erase the effects of constantly doing.

On returning to the boardroom, images and ideas of *ma* in our heads, we were going to make a collagraph which is a type of printing plate made up of collaged elements, but it doesn't withstand many prints as it breaks down over time. In fact, the process felt like a metaphor for a life!

We covered a small, thick, rectangular piece of card with strips of masking tape. It didn't have to be perfect. The edges of tape were to be overlaid, one strip on top of another. Roughly torn edges. No right or wrong way of doing it. No expectations. Only process. We weren't reminded of any outcomes. Just directed through the different stages of making.

I drew branches with spaces in between them directly onto the masking tape-covered card and lightly cut along these lines to gently peel back the first paper layer of card. This would make an indent from which I would later ink up the 'plate' and take a print.

Making simple collagraphs, adding foraged bits of nature from the walk, completely absorbed us for the whole morning. We forgot what time it was and I didn't want to break it up by having to eat lunch. Sometimes hardly speaking to one another, then other times (around cups of tea!) we chatted and laughed. It was a lovely feeling to be part of a group again. Working side by side in good company, seeing the individuality of expression was fascinating. No stress or pressure to talk or compare.

The process was surprising with elements of chance ever-present. Engaging, intriguing, magical and relaxing! There was the right balance between ease, effort and physical activity. For most of the day, I worked standing up and moved between different stations for different materials to use. So different from a desk job! Someone said, "I wish I could be you, Louise, and do this all day!"

Once it had all come to an end, the sense of achievement and positivity did enhance the way I felt. It felt great that I had taken time out for myself, guilt-free, to release those feelings of being stuck. After five sessions, energy felt moving again … because I had tried a different process to what I would normally do, there were even more possibilities to explore. Every Friday I looked forward to coming back to new friends and to new activities.

I cannot express this enough, especially for artists working within the community, just how important it is to carve a creative space for yourself outside of normal day-to-day activities. Make time to give yourself the chance to 'play' so that your enthusiasm and energy is there again for you and finally, if you can do this within the company of a lovely group like this one, all the better.

Box 7.2 Creation – a poem inspired by a staff member's story

Psithurism

We can't see wind, only the things it moves.
Likewise, we can't hear wind
unless it's flowing past something that makes it vibrate;
this causes it to adopt various sonic guises depending on what it interacts with.

Trees provide some of the most common and admired ways for wind to make itself heard.

This sound has been termed psithurism (*sith-err-iz-um*).

The naturalist author and founding member of the RSPB, W.H. Hudson, describes the sound of wind in the trees as 'very restorative' – a mysterious voice which the forest speaks to us, and that to lie or sit thus for an hour at a time listening to the wind is an experience worth going far to seek.

'Through the Trees' project reflection: Rachel

Joining in with art, sharing space, feeling welcomed. Doing creative things because I feel I have a need to do that and being able to do that and find the space to do that.

Draw things, instead of having to talk about things, lose yourself in the doing. Being reminded that I'm pretty much normal, feeling better for it.

It helps to count the things that can't be counted. Lifts my spirits and gives my body a bit of peace to get on with getting better.

Gives time and space enough to be still enough to reorientate my being. A bit like a Google map.

Making new friends, good to have friends.

Learning new things.

Box 7.3 Rookwood – the place

A recent visitor to Rookwood Hospital expressed it very well when she said that the moment she went through the gates and made her way through the grounds she could just feel the peace of the place. It was not bustling or busy or stressed, but relaxed and peaceful. The trees that surround the hospital are an integral part of the place and help provide that peace. It has been the perfect environment for rehabilitation and healing, throughout both world wars and then since the fifties, as a hospital for long-term rehabilitation.

Laughter, stories, colour, time, old-fashioned way of becoming more fully human.

A gateway out of your circumstances.

Offers a connection with other people on a deeper level.

There is a lot of quiet and it's not awkward.

'Through the Trees' project reflection: Janet

It was wet and cold and drizzling, my ankle hurt, I had just recently fallen down the stairs and sprained it. I did not want to go and see the trees. I wanted to sit in the warm and have a coffee and feel sorry for myself. That was the start of a rather magical journey 'through the trees' for me.

It is odd now looking back how it all began and how despite my self-pity I kept returning. I did not see then the beautiful chapel with an amazing sense of peace and stillness or the warm wooden seats. As I looked around at the strange conglomerate of people attending the workshop I tried to do a friendly smile but it was so hard.

Louise was loving and encouraging, suggesting I perhaps just look at the nearest trees – the majestic Wellingtonias. I stood there and looked; I did not feel impressed despite their size. Louise was saying something about the *ma*, the space between the branches; it did not quite make sense to me but between the branches was less dark; there was some light reaching me from between them despite it being a grey day. Louise encouraged us to pick up twigs, leaves etc that tickled our imaginations; I did not pick up any.

We returned to the boardroom which despite being a little dark felt warm and when I sat at the long table with a coffee I felt as if I could be comfortable there forever. Louise was encouraging everyone and showing them how to undertake the artwork and some examples she had made. Everyone seemed so enthusiastic, smiling and keen. They were all very patient with me, showing concern for my fall and sympathy for the pain I must be in. At this point I started to feel guilty as whilst my ankle looked very purple and swollen the pain was not that bad. Others offered me leaves and twigs they had picked up and we began working on cutting out pictures of the things we had collected so we could do some simple prints.

I could not help myself; as much as I wanted to sit and grumble, I found myself becoming engaged in the task as well as interacting with the others. By the end of the day I found myself tired but feeling comfortable with the others in the group and as my creations were put on the table with the others, I felt I also belonged to the group. I wasn't experiencing this on my own.

That was the beginning of my journey. Each time I attended I felt part of the group and I think they may even have begun to like me. My creations were not as artistic as the others; they were more skilled than me, but I actually took pleasure in their achievements. More surprisingly when the exhibition was put together my work did not stand as being too bad next to theirs and people said how much they liked it. That may be true, but I could easily see the artistic abilities of the others.

It wasn't my creations that made the workshops wonderful, it was more to do with the people and the place. I was comfortable to do and say what I felt, without fear; what I did and did not know was not important. It was about being with people who accepted me for who I am but also the alone times. I sat for some time in the chapel which is beautiful and calm, offering a sense of peace. The chapel seemed to glorify nature with lots of animal wooden carving in the architrave and flowers in the ceramic tiles. The little wooden seats were comfortable and warm and when the sun shone it lit up the room.

At the end of the workshops we went for a walk along the tree trail, my ankle no longer causing me a problem. I saw the trees differently; they were awesome, the Wellingtonias strong and majestic, the yews eerie and foreboding, the monkey puzzle tree tall and funny, the magnolia like a pretty ballerina making a curtsey. Yet the tree that seemed most in keeping with me was the mulberry. The mulberry is quite brittle and sensitive, so bits easily fall off and it becomes misshaped. In the early spring all that could be seen was the brittle misshaped branches and twigs but in the early summer it had changed. Now it had its leaves and some tiny flowers, you could not see how misshapen it was. It was now a tree, stood apart from the others but definitely one of them.

Evaluations of 'Through the Trees'

- Absolutely brilliant work
- Lovely thank you
- A blast of nature, informative storytelling in one beautiful trail of trees
- Time, love, care, nature
- What an inspirational 'Tree Walk'. The silver sketchers and I were doing research for our 'Roots' project. Thank you
- This is a wonderful place of hope and healing, of love and laughter
- It's been an absolute pleasure of joy to be part of 'Through the Trees'. Thank you so much
- Joining in with art, sharing space, feeling welcomed. Doing creative things because I feel I have a need to do that and being able to do that and find the space to do that. Draw things, instead of having to talk about things, lose yourself in the doing. Being reminded that I'm pretty much normal, feeling better for it
- What a place! You can feel tremendous history in the boardroom, and it is a privilege to take part in an art workshop here at Rookwood Hospital, especially since it is soon to close. This is the best workshop I have ever attended. I have learnt a variety of printing processes, that have produced

some wonderful pieces of work. Engrossing, fun processes and lovely results, therapy indeed! Jane

- It's a great therapy for artists – to fill the well. We need to re-charge, try new things and then we can go and give again
- Every time I run a project, I feel myself grow, as an artist, as a person. And my hope is that everyone in the group might feel the same. The work we produce is a gift to be treasured, because of the journey we have had together

Creation: Green Pyjamas

A Victorian lady called this place Rookwood
But actually it was ebony birds in flight that bestowed the name.

I was seduced through the trees by your seclusion, your fall, your silence,
By your inconsistent lines and how they dabbled with the light –
A profusion of chinks and shafts superimposing and teasing.
A broken thing, beautiful to an eye such as mine spellbound
By your negative space laced luxuriantly with shadows of laurel, yew and lime.
Too patiently to be seen, nature was embalming you in green bandages
As I stood enamoured.
Maybe she is granting you a stab at eternity.
The gothic vault of your bowels muttered dankly that this should be possible.
I have no doubt the walls of that chamber will outlive the outline of my years.
Indeed, you have the privilege of a preservation order.
I wonder how that feels.
However, it does not cover your un-architectured harmony –
Your stone meeting leaf, your beam meeting branch and your light meeting shadow.
Thank you for greeting me informally in your green pyjamas.

You prompted the return of my ten-year-old eyes,
And they skipped across your hidden contours – your playground just out of reach –
Marvelling at how the fencing and scaffolding
Had been absorbed into your present aesthetic.
You have relaxed towards a more organic manifestation.
The neatness of your octagonal inception has given way to a more interesting state –
A wondrous new integrity, a lounging rather than a standing.
A folly has no mission

But is designed to make a statement – a kind of ta-dah, this is me
But now there is more of a yawn and a laid back I am here in this wooded place.
I am glad I can only glimpse you through the trees, glad that I am fenced out
And that the tendrils of my imagination alone can enter.

Jane Lewis, inspired by the Summerhouse and Vaulted Chamber, dating back to the thirteenth century, and resurrected at Rookwood Hospital, April 2019

Creations: Watercolour monoprints

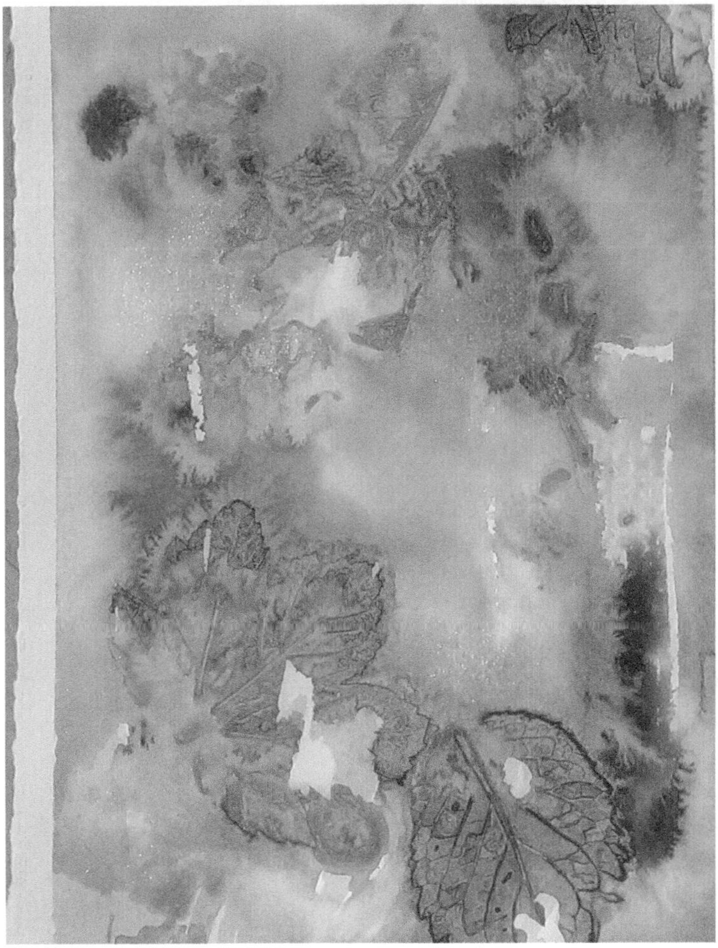

Figure 7.3 Marion's watercolour monoprint.

Figure 7.4 Steve's watercolour monoprint.

Creation: The Wellingtonia

Seconds tick by
quietly making rings.
An ancient mammoth girth
resting and weighing, descending
deeper into the earth's silted layers.
The bone-white root
way, way down
sends one of its fingers
just a little further

Stretching high
the topmost leaf cavorts in a gun-grey sky
tugged by an unkind wind
frilled edges whipping
a wild, reeling arc

After hours
the squall vanishes
day darkening to silhouette
against a chalk moon

Rooks stay quiet in the sharpened air
not sleeping

Louise Jensen, Rookwood Hospital, November 2018

Creation: Wellingtonia linocut – Louise

Figure 7.5 Louise's Wellingtonia linocut.

Creations: Foil relief prints

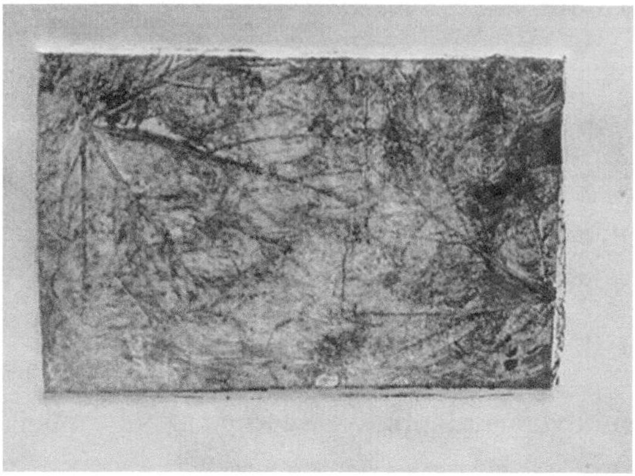

Figure 7.6 Rachel's sycamore foil relief.

Figure 7.7 Jane's foil relief.

Creation: A poem in response to Rookwood

Tryst

Lithe limbs of light
entwine
with lithe limbs of bough.
The above romances
the below
in a sylvan cathedral
of chiaroscuro.

Waking breath of sky
commingles
with dreaming breath of wood –
so many kisses
in the mist –
the language of dawn
is silently understood.

Creation collage

Figure 7.8 Marion's collage.

Summary

This chapter has offered a selection of evaluations, reflections, pictures and creative writing. It starts with a review of the Collingwood project called Artist in the Making. Those involved felt privileged to have access to the amazing and intimate Collingwood Archive. The evaluations identify a number of features that were important to the participants; these were:

- More satisfied with life, more happiness
- Creations
- Opportunity to learn
- Company of others
- Time to focus

These can all be found in the literature such as the Department of Health, Diener and Suh and Ryff, as indicated earlier, but a couple of other features appear poignant to this group and they were freedom and time to engage with warmth and positivity.

The second project explored in the chapter is the 'Through the Trees' project based at Rookwood Hospital. The evaluations offered the same features identified in the literature above, but the sense of privilege appears to be more associated with place rather than difficult to access and intimate family materials. The 'Through the Trees' project also had additional characteristics:

- Love, care and hope
- Time for silence and laughter
- Engaging, intriguing, magical and relaxing

Conclusions

Both projects were led by Louise and structured in a similar way and therefore the main differences in the projects were focus, time and place. This can be found not only in the evaluation but in the reflections as well. The reflections have been left as the individual's written stories so that the reader can draw out their own interpretations and meanings. It is hoped that the reader will find the understanding of an embodied self and acceptance of self and others as a feature of mental wellbeing which was apparent to the authors, but they leave the reader to develop, in turn, their own story.

Despite a lack of interpretation offered here it is clear that the phenomenon of mental wellbeing is an embodied experience within a certain sense of time and place that can be enlivened by creativity but is more complex than a simple scientific definition can offer.

References

Cameron, J. 1994. *The Artist's Way: A Course in Discovering and Rediscovering Your Creative Self.* London: Souvenir Press.

Department of Health (DoH). 2007. Commissioning Framework for Health and Wellbeing, p. 99. www.visionuk.org.uk/download/archive_1/pdf/PDF%20health%20and%20well(1).pdf

Diener, E., Suh, E. 1997. "Measuring Quality of Life: Economic, Social, and Subjective Indicators", *Social Indicators Research*, 40, 1–2, 189–216. DOI: http://dx.doi.org/10.1023/A:1006859511756.

HM Gov. 2010. Our Health and Wellbeing Today. https://assets.publishing.service.gov.uk/government/uploads/system/uploads/attachment_data/file/215911/dh_122238.pdf.

McGrath, J., 2018. The Japanese Words for "space" Could Change Your View of the World. https://qz.com/1181019/the-japanese-words-for-space-could-change-your-view-of-the-world/.

Plucker, J.A., Beghetto, R.A., Dow, G.T. 2004. "Why Isn't Creativity More Important to Educational Psychologists? Potentials, Pitfalls, and Future Directions in Creativity Research", *Educational Psychologist*, 39, 2, 83–96.

Ryff, C.D. 1989. "Happiness Is Everything, or Is It? Explorations on the Meaning of Psychological Wellbeing", *Journal of Personality and Social Psychology*, 57, 1069–1081. DOI: http://dx.doi.org/10.1037/00223514.57.6.1069.

Chapter 8

Phenomenological psychological lifeworld experiences

Introduction

This book has led the reader on a journey from an introductory chapter offering the context and rationale for the book to exploring each relevant concept in separate chapters leading to a description of the activities undertaken by the Stiwdio Arts Group. This concluded with Chapter 7 focusing on the evaluations, reflections and outputs of the group and in Chapter 8, this chapter, there will be an 'unpicking' of these and an offering of some practical suggestions for future practice.

The following reflection from one of the members of the 'Through the Trees' project spells out rather poetically the essence of the undertakings of the Stiwdio Arts Group:

> Joining in with art, sharing space, feeling welcomed.
> Doing creative things because I feel I have a need to do that and being able to do that and find the space to do that.
> Draw things, instead of having to talk about things, lose yourself in the doing.
> Being reminded that I'm pretty much normal, feeling better for it.
> It helps to count the things that can't be counted.
> Lifts my spirits and gives my body a bit of peace to get on with getting better
> Gives time and space enough to be still enough to reorientate my being.
> A bit like a Google map.
> Making new friends, good to have friends
> Learning new things
> Laughter, stories, colour, time, old-fashioned way of becoming more fully human
> A gateway out of your circumstances
> Offers a connection with other people on a deeper level
> There is a lot of quiet and it's not awkward

As highlighted by gestalt theorists, there is more to the whole than the sum of the parts whether a poem, an activity, an experience or concept and this is certainly true of this reflective poem. This has been the 'truth' behind all explorations of concepts in this book. Psychological phenomenology, with its recognition of the centrality of fully realised 'lifeworld experiences', accepting concepts such as 'soulful space' and 'felt sense', guides researchers to look beyond the measurable, objective scientific approach. They are led to ask what is the 'lived experience' of the phenomenon and how can we understand using all ways of knowing.

As philosophically interesting as this is, what remains a concern for health and social care services and individual practitioners is, how does this type of understanding guide our endeavours and justify our use of limited resources? Whole reflections and poems (including artworks) were provided in Chapter 7 which can be digested and uniquely perceived by the reader but the authors are attempting, in this chapter, to offer examples that remain true to the meaning of the initial stories but can be examined alongside previous understandings. It offers a way of being, ontology to developing understanding of knowledge, epistemology.

Mental wellbeing

Wellbeing was explored in Chapter 2 in which was provided an understanding of the importance of mental wellbeing, its place in contemporary culture and the literature currently available. Given the link between mental wellbeing and health, the first definition provided was from the Department of Health (2007: 99) in the UK whose definition was:

> Well-being is the subjective state of being healthy, happy, contented, comfortable and satisfied with one's quality of life. It includes physical, material, social, emotional ('happiness'), and development and activity dimensions.

Whilst this appears a clear and concise definition, Thomas (2009) still believed wellbeing is intangible and difficult to define. He also argued it is even harder to measure. This is mostly due to the lack of clarity of the concepts within the definition such as 'health', 'comfort' and 'quality of life' as well as the boundaries of subjectivity. Leading on from this definition and after further exploration, the following was developed in an attempt to achieve more clarity:

> On consideration of contemporary literature subjective wellbeing (or personal wellbeing) is how people think and feel about their own wellbeing and includes aspects such as life satisfaction (evaluation), positive emotions (hedonic), and whether life is meaningful (eudaemonic).

There remain, though, problems with these elements or dimensions, in fact with any division of wellbeing philosophically, due to the differing values attached to them which influences how they are experienced. Consider, for example, the dichotomy between hedonists and moral or value-based motivations. Despite whether positive emotions or moral values are the basis for securing wellbeing, high self-esteem, personal control and sense of identity improve subjective wellbeing for Eastern cultures as well as Western ones. Low self-esteem, even though humility is a valued attribute for many, does not appear to be associated with wellbeing in any culture.

Whilst blurring within and around the concept of wellbeing is evident, anthropologists highlight the need to recognise a multiplicity of 'wellbeings' and the importance of place or context (Mathews and Izquierdo 2009). Alongside place and context contemporary culture also promotes the need for an acceptance of different types of wellbeing. For many cultures the spirituality or faith of the society provides a strong context for wellbeing. Spiritually within Islamic and Christian societies there is a focus on forgiveness and removal of guilt (shalom) to gain peace, deep joy – wellbeing. For Buddhist societies balance within life is required as suffering is intrinsic to living and for Hindus wellbeing is achieved through appropriateness of behaviour which again is dependent on context (see Chapter 2 for more detail).

Shalom is key to wellbeing for Jews, Christians and Muslims, influenced by a relationship with God (theist); for Buddhists happiness is key (hedonist) which is the individual's responsibility and within their control. For Hindus personal responsibility and control (value driven or categorical imperative) are also dictators of their destiny, as Karma leads to the person experiencing, in their next life, the consequences of behaviour in their current incarnation.

Alongside definitions of the concept of wellbeing from health and anthropology (culture including faith), each of the psychological perspectives offers a different understanding of wellbeing too. These are mostly associated with a more traditional scientific approach (see Chapter 2 for details). Box 8.1 offers an overview of the key dimensions considered so far.

Psychodynamic theorists recognise wellbeing as balancing (by the ego) of the opposing parts of the mind (id and superego) which is developed through close relationships with others. Relationships are key for the humanists too. They state that for a person to become who they are meant to be they need to receive unconditional positive regard from another, which is usually gained in early life from parents.

Social interaction, which might be recognised as relationships, is key for behaviourists, but the process, for them, is quite different. People need role models or others to condition their behaviour, so that they can learn how to be most efficient in achieving adaptive behaviours i.e. wellbeing. For many people behavioural approaches, particularly classical and operant conditioning, are considered unethical for use with the general public despite their extensive use within health (for example placebos), childcare (for example

Box 8.1 Keys to mental wellbeing

Philosophy

Hedonism
Moral, ethical value based

Religion

Forgiveness and removal of guilt (shalom) to gain peace, deep joy
Balance within life
Appropriateness of behaviour

Contemporary literature

Life satisfaction (evaluation), positive emotions (hedonic) and whether life is meaningful (eudaemonic)

Psychology

Balancing and relationships
Unconditional positive regard
Social conditioning
Positive emotions, engagement, relationships, meaning and purpose, accomplishment

star charts) and education (for example awards). Social learning theory is, though, more acceptable to Western societies as role models, buddies, mentors etc are widely recommended within the professions.

Cognitive, behavioural and positive psychologists have all sought to develop specific psychological models to understand and measure wellbeing. They have produced tools for measurement of wellbeing from generic self-report questionnaires to ones that focus on specific dimensions of wellbeing such as those identified in Box 8.2.

Despite the literature, including Buddhist spirituality, stating a need for balance in life, within the evaluations and reflections in Chapter 7 there was only one statement related to balance and that referred to physical activity, not from a psychological or philosophical perspective:

> There was the right balance between ease, effort and physical activity.

All the other dimensions highlighted in Box 8.2 were mentioned in these evaluations and reflections (see Table 8.1 for some examples). The artwork provides clues as to the importance of the dimensions at a more implicit, intuitive, perceptual level.

Box 8.2 Dimension of mental wellbeing from this current exploration

For most people one or more of these elements are an important aspect of their mental wellbeing:

- Happiness
- Appropriate behaviour
- Forgiveness
- Balance
- Satisfaction
- Meaning
- Relationship
- Warmth
- Learning
- Accomplishment

Table 8.1 Examples of dimensions from evaluations, reflections and poems

Dimension	*Quote*	*Project*
Happiness	Enjoyable, felt like I could make and finish something	Collingwood evaluation
Appropriate behaviour	I could not help myself, as much I as I wanted to sit and grumble, I found myself becoming engaged in the task as well as interacting with the others	'Through the Trees' reflection
Forgiveness	When I arrived, everyone smiled at me and showed concern about my getting lost again	Collingwood reflection
Balance	There was the right balance between ease, effort and physical activity	'Through the Trees' evaluation
Satisfaction	More satisfied with life, more happiness	Collingwood evaluation
Meaning	Laughter, stories, colour, time, old-fashioned way of becoming more fully human	'Through the Trees' reflection
Relationship	Being part of the group and enjoying the activity, getting in touch and socialising	Collingwood evaluation
Warmth	Time to focus on positive, warm and comforting about people and history, which makes me feel warmer and more comfortable	Collingwood evaluation

Dimension	*Quote*	*Project*
Learning	It's about not taking the unsuccessful moments as failures, but about being ready to pick up and start again having learnt the lessons	'Through the Trees' reflection
Accomplishment	Having something nice that I had made at the end of the project and seeing other people do the same	Collingwood evaluation

Flourishing

The positivist psychologist's exploration of wellbeing led them to rename the concept as the established understanding did not fulfil their expectations from a positivist perspective (see Chapter 2). Eudaemonia is commonly translated as 'wellbeing' but more accurately translates as 'human flourishing' or 'prosperity'. Therefore, the positive psychologists use the term flourishing instead of wellbeing to distance their exploration from the previously established literature.

In Chapter 5 mental wellbeing was identified by Keyes and Seligman (positive psychologists) as *flourishing* which they stated was a new and dynamic approach. For them mental wellbeing or flourishing occurs when a person can reach their unique potential. Despite being proposed as a new and dynamic approach it has distinct similarities to Rogers' aim for his clients: to become themself. Keyes' and Seligman's models are, though, more cognitive behavioural in flavour than humanistic, but they do highlight that human relationships and a sense of meaning are key to wellbeing.

Tay *et al.* (2018) believed that creative arts and humanities may strengthen aspects of human flourishing, such as character, values, civic engagement and morality. Given the focus on achievements related to morals, values and ethics, Tay *et al.*'s philosophical base appears to have its foundations in the work of Socrates and could be labelled axiology. They offer a conceptual framework for the role of the arts and humanities in human flourishing. It consists of the 'what' and 'how' of the art or humanity and the mechanisms that lead to human flourishing outcomes. Their mechanisms to gain wellbeing are immersion, embeddedness, socialisation and reflection (Tay *et al.* 2018). These four mechanisms appear to have little in common with the dimensions identified in this book, but the mechanisms are identified as processes to achieve the dimensions (attribute, evaluation, emotion or prize). For some participants in the Stiwdio Arts Group the process itself led to a sense of mental wellbeing:

> It didn't have to be perfect. The edges of tape were to be overlaid, one strip on top of another. Roughly torn edges. No right or wrong way of doing it. No expectations. Only process. We weren't reminded of any outcomes. Just directed through the different stages of making.

Understanding and thinking creatively like this allows people to be more open and aware of experiences of self, others and culture, which supports social interaction and deeper relationships to develop and, as stated by Wright and Pascoe (2015), a fuller sense of humanity.

Whilst researchers and those providing the funding for them may be concerned with public values, civic engagement and morals this does not seem to be a feature of importance to participants of the Stwidio Arts projects. The evaluations from the Collingwood Stiwdio Arts project identified the following as significant achievements of the experience:

- More satisfied with life, more happiness
- Creations
- Opportunity to learn
- Company of others
- Time to focus

These can all be found in the literature such as the DoH, Diener and Suh, and Ryff, but a couple of other features appeared poignant to this group, which were freedom and time to engage with warmth and positivity.

The 'Through the Trees' project evaluations offered the same features as identified above, but their sense of privilege is more associated with place rather than objects, the difficult to access and intimate family archives. The physical environment can also be seen to support group functioning and flourishing as indicated by the following quote:

> Louise introduced the project in a friendly, unassuming yet knowledgeable way. She had meticulously laid the room out. Absolutely everything we could possibly need was there and within easy reach. It must have taken ages to prepare.

This project's evaluations also had additional characteristics:

- Love, care and hope
- Time for silence and laughter
- Engaging, intriguing, magical and relaxing

All these features occurred in the reflections and creative writing from the participants too. The whole experience of the group members was something 'more' than the elements established in previous literature. The key to understanding mental wellbeing, given the findings in Chapter 7 along with understanding gained from philosophy, anthropology and psychology, is *through lived experiences of shared joy mediated by the body, truth, beauty and/or the divine; this makes suffering in life experiences meaningful and life worthwhile.*

Self

Given the accepted subjectivity of mental wellbeing, the concept of embodied subjective self was explored in Chapter 3 starting with a consideration of the objective or social self: personality. Using a cognitive behavioural perspective self or personality can be defined as the relatively stable traits or characteristics demonstrated by a person over time. This understanding of self can be seen in the reflections gained from the Stiwdio Arts Group; see below.

> "This level of anxiety and stress is ever-present no matter what kind of work I do. Other people might say, "You care too much …" but I can't help it."
>
> "Whether or not I can work creatively is somewhere completely bound up in this sense of worthlessness."
>
> "Reflecting on my own bouts of depression I know that when I disintegrate into them it is with a tortured lack of self-esteem. I feel of no consequence, can see no value to what I am or what I do. There is a blindly subjective feeling of spiralling inwards, painfully spiralling down into a state of non-existence."

If anxiety, as in the quotes above, is believed to be a personality trait that is relatively stable over time then the situation for these participants would appear to offer limited hope. A humanistic existential philosophy, which indicates people have control over their own destinies and choose their behaviour, may be also be problematic; it could be experienced as condemning. A bio-psychosocial approach is more helpful for the individual due to the recognition of the interaction of the person's biology, psychology and social situation all influencing the person's experience. It offers more hope in that if one of these areas could be changed the anxiety may be alleviated.

Certainly, cognitive behavioural therapy has been found to be effective in management of diagnosed anxiety disorders. It is proposed here, though, that a recognition of an embodied subjective self within a psychological phenomenological perspective offers greater opportunity for flourishing and mental wellbeing. Self-recognition and acceptance of one's self including vulnerability may be the first step towards self-compassion and mental wellbeing.

Mental wellbeing is acknowledged as having social or relational elements but the participants in the Stiwdio Arts Group, in their evaluations, reflections and creative writing, also indicated the relevance of their embodied subjective self. Subjective self is a personal understanding of who I am which is embodied; where the body shapes the mind, ideas forming through bodily experiences. It can be recognised in the following quote from one of the participants:

> This push back is a practical, searching, curious drive that reaches out to speak to other people and asks to be seen, however modestly and asks to be of some agency in the world.

The way in which people experience and develop their embodied knowledge is through their 'felt sense' (see Chapter 3). Felt sense is different from emotional feelings; it is a bodily awareness of living and ongoing life processes. Felt sense is a living interaction with the world. The more people are in tune with their felt sense, their experience of being alive in the world, the greater their opportunity for wellbeing. In the following quotes are indications of a retrospective recognition of beauty and wonder which in the moment were overshadowed by the pressure of anxiety and mood. In the second quote there are signs of hope in the identification of *ma* in the trees.

> "I did not see then the beautiful chapel with an amazing sense of peace and stillness or the warm wooden seats. As I looked around at the strange conglomerate of people attending the workshop I tried to do a friendly smile but it was so hard."

> "I stood there and looked; I did not feel impressed despite their size. Louise was saying something about the *ma*, the space between the branches, it did not quite make sense to me but between the branches was less dark, there was some light reaching me from between them despite it being a grey day."

As the participants moved through the workshops their acknowledgement and engagement with their felt sense became more apparent and their relationships became more supportive and relaxed, facilitating their positive expressions (see quotes below).

> "I was very pleased with my success and strangely I didn't need everyone to say how good it was."

> "… draw things, instead of having to talk about things, lose yourself in the doing."

> "Engrossing, fun processes and lovely results, therapy indeed!"

> "Once it had all come to an end, the sense of achievement and positivity did enhance the way I felt. It felt great that I had taken time out for myself, guilt-free to release those feelings of being stuck. After five sessions, energy felt moving again … because I had tried a different process to what I would normally do, there were even more possibilities to explore. Every Friday I looked forward to coming back to new friends and to new activities."

> "It's a great therapy for artists – to fill the well. We need to re-charge, try new things and then we can go and give again."

> "Yet the tree that seemed most in keeping with me was the mulberry. The mulberry is quite brittle and sensitive, so bits easily fall off and it becomes misshaped. In the early spring all that could be seen was the brittle misshaped branches and twigs but in the early summer it had changed. Now it had its leaves and some tiny flowers, you could not see how misshapen it was. It was now a tree, stood apart from the others but definitely one of them."

The quote above may be an indication that the participant is developing an awareness of their personal 'soulful space' (see Chapter 4): the ability to enter a moment in time and space where they can accept themselves, in their entirety, including their vulnerability, to have a deep sense of who they are and who they are becoming.

Dwelling mobility

Meaning in life (eudaemonia) has been highlighted in the literature as of relevance to mental wellbeing. Keyes and Seligman's models among others highlight human relationships and a sense of meaning as being key to mental wellbeing. Ryan and Deci (2001) state that eudaemonia focuses on individuals' meaningful engagement in life. It is dynamic, culturally defined and determined; it is where creativity and learning are intertwined and what is felt or sensate is always present. Those not experiencing eudaemonia are not aware or engaged with their 'felt sense'. For life to have the most fulfilling meaning the person needs to be open to the full extent of their lifeworld experiences including their felt sense. This can be achieved in a number of ways such as focusing, which will be explored later in the chapter.

Tay *et al.*'s (2018) framework of human flourishing (which has been labelled wellbeing or eudaemonia) through the mechanisms of immersion, embeddedness, socialisation and reflectiveness, as described in Chapter 5, also provides a process for the development of creativity. Their framework offers a tool for future exploration and understanding using traditional scientific research methods. Alongside Tay *et al.*'s framework Ryan and Deci's mechanisms of relational, self-realisation and meaningful engagement appear to offer a similar foundation for flourishing or eudaemonia using different but associated terms. Whilst Tay *et al.*'s mechanisms can be defined cognitively Ryan and Deci's mechanisms are more sensate where eudaemonia is achieved through Gendlin's and Geurts and Adikha's 'felt sense'; a bodily awareness of living and ongoing life processes. An engagement with felt sense can be identified in the following quotes from the Stiwdio Arts Group.

> "… it was a more visceral experience."
> "I found the whole experience moving."

Felt sense is a living interaction with the world. The more people are in tune with their felt sense, their experience of being alive in the world, the greater their opportunity for wellbeing. A felt sense is clearly seen in the Stiwdio Arts Group's expressions of their experiences through words such as *'magical', 'love', 'warmth', intriguing', 'hope'*.

Todres (2004), based on the need to engage with one's felt sense, developed the concept of 'soulful space' (see Chapter 4). This is the ability to access a 'soulful space', a moment in time and space where the person can accept themselves, in their entirety, including their vulnerability. This leads to gaining a deep sense of who they are and who they are becoming which facilitates the experience of mental wellbeing. The following quotes may demonstrate a person moving towards a soulful space and dwelling mobility.

> "I could not help myself, as much as I wanted to sit and grumble, I found myself becoming engaged in the task as well as interacting with the others. By the end of the day I found myself tired but feeling comfortable with the others in the group and as my creations were put on the table with the others, I felt I also belonged to the group. I wasn't experiencing this on my own."

> "It was wonderful to be able to focus on something pretty. I liked to think about Ursula being encouraged by her mother to draw and paint sitting in pretty Edwardian clothes in the sunshine overlooking the lake. It was as if I was taking on some of her experiences, I started to feel more feminine and pretty. I felt as if instead of being in that small cold art room I was there by the lake with her, a loving and encouraging mother, warm sunshine, feeling confident and happy."

These quotes appear psychologically humanistic and philosophically existentialist and whilst Todres is influenced by these ideas he also recognised the need for others: relationships. He states that inclusive empathy (the understanding of others) supports and is supported by a synchronous intersubjective temporality (interacting harmoniously in a particular time). For Todres, philosophically, the conception of temporal and spatial subjectivity and intersubjective experiences provide a platform for self-understanding and wellbeing. He has identified wellbeing as having two elements, he states wellbeing is both a way of being-in-the-world and a felt sense of what this is like as an experience, which he calls dwelling mobility (Todres and Galvin 2010). The development of the concept of dwelling mobility was based on the Heideggerian philosophical approach to homelessness. Dwelling mobility may be of use in unpacking reflections, evaluations, definitions and creative writing provided in this book.

Dwelling and mobility are opposing poles along a construct one is about being still and the other about movement. For Todres and Galvin (2010) they also use the terms peace and movement but dwelling and mobility are said to be more encompassing, wider concepts, to explore the phenomenon of wellbeing. They suggest a person can experience both opposing existential and metaphorical possibilities of these concepts, a harmony, at the same time to gain a sense of wellbeing. The sense of being-at-home of rootedness and peace can occur at the same time as being aware of possible adventure. Todres and Galvin (2010:5) state,

> The essence of mobility lies in all the ways in which we are called into the existential possibilities of moving forward with time, space, others, mood and our bodies. The feeling of this "moving forward" is one of energised flow.
>
> The essence of dwelling lies in all the ways that we existentially "come home" to what we have been given in time, space, others, mood and our bodies. The feeling of this "coming home" is one of acceptance, "rootedness" and "peace".

Philosophers such as Gendlin, Todres, Tilley and Malpas all identify that there is more to an experience than can be summed up by what can be seen and measured. The rich tapestry of life can only be appreciated by embodied self-recognition and interaction with the world including a recognition that experiences occur in time and space. As part of this, mental wellbeing occurs through acceptance of self and others within a state of temporal and spatial dwelling mobility.

Temporality: engagement with past and present

History enables discovery and understanding in the recorded past and for the time before the opportunity to write was available archaeology offers a route to learning and understanding. Whilst in the Stiwdio Arts projects there was an opportunity to explore the relevant archives, more was gained than could be rationally expected from the written words and the contents of archived creations. The group participants appear to have been able to engage with their felt sense and access their dwelling mobility to engage at a soulful level with the materials. The participants all made comments reflecting the impact the archives had on them:

> "Time to focus on positive; warm and comforting about people and history, which makes me feel warmer and more comfortable"
>
> "To be able to view the tiny beautiful pictures and to gain awareness of how it was to live in the nineteenth century"

> "a wonderful window into the whole culture of their family life and creative work"
>
> "I loved the tiny pictures of animals drawn by the children and felt rather drawn to Ursula the youngest daughter. She seemed to be her own person and the least artistic"
>
> "I was drawn very specifically to Edith Collingwood, and her role as a home-school teacher. I was drawn to the children and the work they had produced as children, and I was curious to know how they had turned out, and if there was a connection with this way of teaching them in their early years"

The importance of access to archives, historical artefacts and environments are well recorded by Historic England who state that they protect, champion and save places that define who we are. As part of their heritage framework (see Table 8.2) they outline awareness and engagement with history personally (ancestry, genealogy, identity, values, ownership) or publicly (culture, customs, traditions, values, national treasures).

Understanding of ancestry is considered essential to understanding ourselves and our basic humanity and diversity. As Nicholson states, "It informs our sense of identity and place in contemporary culture, geographical and historical space" (2018: 29).

Table 8.2 Heritage framework linked to wellbeing and Stiwdio Arts projects

Feature	*Quote*	*Project*
Process	Being part of the group and enjoying the activity	Collingwood evaluation
Participation	I didn't realise just how important taking part would be and how it would make me feel …	'Through the Trees' reflection
Mechanism	Making simple collagraphs, adding foraged bits of nature from the walk completely absorbed us for the whole morning	'Through the Trees' reflection
Healing	This is a wonderful place of hope and healing, of love and laughter	'Through the Trees' evaluation
Place	What a place! You can feel tremendous history in the boardroom, and it is a privilege to take part in an art workshop here at Rookwood Hospital, especially since it is soon to close	'Through the Trees' reflection
Environment	With the archives laid out it was as if we were revering it; we all appeared in awe and respectful of what was laid out in front of us	Collingwood reflection

Interpersonal relationships moderate the effect of life events and the level of quality of these relationships correlates with the sense of wellbeing (Burns and Machin 2013). As small groups the participants in the Stiwdio Arts projects had the opportunity to get to know each other at a deeper level and support each other. Whilst opportunity was provided there was no guarantee this would happen with a group, but with skilful facilitation using compassionate communication skills (Barker and Williams, 2018), a fertile environment was provided. As can be seen in the quotes from participants, the relationships developed became an important element of their sense of wellbeing.

> "The work we produce is a gift to be treasured, because of the journey we have had together."
>
> "Welcomed with tea and biscuits (never underestimate the power of a cuppa). The group was friendly and diverse."

Friedman (1992), as identified in Chapter 4, established the importance of historical (or temporal), spatial and social determinants of self-identification: self-recognition. Later Fuchs (2013) also acknowledged the importance of these from a phenomenological philosophical perspective described in the same chapter. His description of three features of temporality, implicit subjective temporality, explicit subjective temporality and intersubjective temporality were outlined. Intersubjective temporal synchronicity was identified as being influenced by feedback from the social environment, which is achieved through daily contact with others and becoming attuned through bodily, emotional and interactional communication.

Intersubjective temporality was discussed above in relation to Todres' development of soulful space. Soulful space is the ability to access a moment in time and space where the person can accept themselves, in their entirety, including their vulnerability, to have a deep sense of who they are and who they are becoming. Accepting a 'soulful space' indicates a kind of freedom, a freedom to embrace the whole of oneself, to acknowledge one's full humanity, embodied self-recognition. This sense of freedom was something the project participants also acknowledged, as seen in their quotes:

> "Freedom to do our art as part of project."
>
> "Joining in with art, sharing space, feeling welcomed. Doing creative things because I feel I have a need to do that and being able to do that and find the space to do that."
>
> "Louise seemed to understand and gave me some space."

Todres' (2007) soulful space correlates with Gendlin's (1987) description of a kind of 'flow' of 'being-with' where human vulnerability, need and 'unfinishedness' of oneself is embraced. This is a natural moving from past through the present, accepting the future will bring change which is one part of the dwelling mobility phenomenon. Not only do people need to understand themselves and their personal history but also how this interweaves with their sense of other and other's history.

Inclusive empathy supports and is supported by a synchronous intersubjective temporality. Philosophically the conception of temporal and spatial subjective and intersubjective experiences provides a platform for self-understanding and wellbeing. When these concepts are not acknowledged, dyssynchronous intersubjective experiences could occur, leading to reduced empathy and wellbeing. Todres (2004) states soulfulness offers a place to recognise and accept individual heartfelt historical moments. It includes the things that we are touched by: being open to others and temporality.

Each of the psychological perspectives offers a different understanding of wellbeing but all involve a place or environment to support change and interaction with others despite some leading to individualistic therapeutic approaches.

> "As a group we had gone on a journey of sorts, and we had been creating and working together."
>
> "It was also immensely rewarding to be part of the group."
>
> "I had had a successful day, despite being late and everyone had treated me as if I was normal and did not seem to have any particular expectations of me."

Empathy and synchronicity, whilst occurring between project participants, participants and facilitators, also appeared to occur between the participants and archives where one participant with reference to the Collingwood archive said:

> We felt we had a relationship with them.

Creative interactions with the past and present can awaken understanding and ways of thinking through which is gained a wealth of experiences of self and other. Creative activities based on the past can offer interdependency and recognition, filling life with engagement, meaning and relationships, a richer humanity (Wright and Pascoe 2015).

> It wasn't my creations that made the workshops wonderful, it was more to do with the people and the place. I was comfortable to do and say what I felt, without fear; what I did and did not know was not important.

Intersubjective temporality suggests a shared understanding of time and place; it is relational.

> We stood outside looking at the gardens and he told me how he was struggling with his energy and his ability to think. I know it sounds unkind but it sort of made me feel better; being able to listen to someone else and them wanting to talk to me about something sensitive.

The place and its history are intertwined with humans; it is a two-way relationship. People influence the place and the place influences the person within time.

> "This has been a wonderful place of hope and healing, of love and laughter."
>
> "It's been an absolute pleasure of joy to be part of 'Through the Trees'."
>
> "Being reminded that I'm pretty much normal, feeling better for it."
>
> "The group made me feel safe, secure and comfortable."

Environment, place and context

The same but different – the projects being explored here could be considered the same yet different. The workshops involved being introduced to an archive and learning new creative techniques in a small group with the aim of improving the participants' sense of wellbeing. The most obvious difference was that the archives were stored in different environments and the workshops were undertaken in different locations. Whilst the facilitator was the same, those supporting her were different and there were different participants although some already knew each other.

The environment, the place and the context were something all the participants described in their evaluations, reflections and creative writing. This was obviously an important element in the lived experiences of the projects. The impact of the environment is profound and has a significant effect on a person's sense of wellbeing (Nicholls *et al.* 2015) with Mathews and Izquierdo (2009) stating that the importance of place or context should not be ignored.

The micro-cultures developed by each project became full of shared meanings and experiences and allowed the small distinct groups of people to manage their everyday experiences. This provision for a sense of wellbeing is fundamentally linked to the person's sense of identity within time and place (Barker 2018).

> We had worked on the Collingwoods, peeked into their lives, drawn out our perceptions of them and their work, and begun to understand them as children, as the people they became, and as the artists they were, in the making. As a group we had gone on a journey of sorts, and we had been creating and working together towards our portrait of this family, and in doing so, also positioning ourselves as artists in the making.

An embodied recovery environment, an environment that facilitates a sense of mental wellbeing, is a place or milieu created in time and space where a person can have enough control to experience their whole existential self in a meaningful and hopeful way. They are situated in an environment in which they can recognise who they are whilst feeling accepted and appreciated by those around them.

Artist in the making

The current socio-political context of the project was of concern as indicated in this quote:

> I have been very aware, as has everyone I know, of the social and political context in which the project took place and particularly here in Britain where there has been a sense of a prolonged and painful transition, a not knowing, a lack of solution or of resolution.

The Arts, Humanities and Social Science special collections archive where the Collingwood family archive was stored was an unfamiliar environment for most members of the group along with the presentation of the archive:

> "I felt a bit awestruck, the room was bright and light; it felt air conditioned. There were lots of pieces on display, lots of pictures, post cards and pieces of writing."
>
> "The first time we all met at the library where the archives were stored was a really odd experience. We all stood round a large table with the archives laid out and it was as if we were revering it; we all appeared in awe and respectful of what was laid out in front of us."
>
> "... when seeing what a large and manifold collection it was, a little overwhelmed."
>
> "It was also immensely rewarding to be part of the group, surrounded by such inspiring material and to have the opportunity to work together to create the miniature books."

The physical space where the workshops were undertaken were not commented on in any detail for this project, but the relational aspects and their emotional impact do appear to be significant.

> I was drawn to how she had been with her children, as a mother, as an artist and as an educator. She had annotated their work carefully and kept all of their work in chronological order, noting how they were developing along the way. To me, this was in some ways astounding, and it is for

two reasons. Firstly, because she was giving so much status to the notion and practice of working artistically, and secondly she was giving status to each of the children individually, really reflecting back to them, with a degree of gravity, their agency in the world. What they did, what they had produced mattered.

Through the Trees

The exploration of the Rookwood archive started in the Glamorgan Archives in which a group explored some old scrapbooks, put together by the Hill family. This archive was housed in a large building with impressive safety and security features, but the viewing room was similar to a modern teaching room. This element of the project was not commented on by the participants, but the location of the workshops was widely discussed in all their writings and extensively features in the artwork.

> "Coming to Rookwood was something rather different. I was drawn to the trees, to their silence, to their solidity, and in the first instance during those winter months, their silhouetted beauty against the sky."

> "A recent visitor to Rookwood Hospital expressed it very well when she said that the moment she went through the gates and made her way through the grounds she could just feel the peace of the place. It was not bustling or busy or stressed, but relaxed and peaceful. The trees that surround the hospital are an integral part of the place and help provide that peace. It has been the perfect environment for rehabilitation and healing."

> "Workshops would take place in the boardroom – a huge, darkly gothic room on the ground floor of Rookwood Hospital – a place steeped in history. At one end, large double doors opened out onto the gardens – we were so close to nature and could see the rooks, trees rustling in the wind and hear birdsong."

> "She had meticulously laid the room out. Absolutely everything we could possibly need was there and within easy reach. It must have taken ages to prepare. We went outside for a walk in the hospital grounds. Not for the sake of it, we looked up at trees, in between branches and not down at our phones. We made conversations that weren't about why we were here or what had happened."

> "We were introduced to the Japanese concept of *ma* – the spaces between things. Spaces in between branches, leaves and the air. Spaces to rest. Spaces in between busy-ness and nothing. Spaces to erase the effects of constantly doing."

One of the participants on their first walk around the hospital grounds felt led to write a poem:

> I was seduced through the trees by your seclusion, your fall, your silence,
> By your inconsistent lines and how they dabbled with the light –
> A profusion of chinks and shafts superimposing and teasing.
> A broken thing, beautiful to an eye such as mine spellbound
> By your negative space laced luxuriantly with shadows of laurel, yew and lime.
> Too patiently to be seen, nature was embalming you in green bandages
> As I stood enamoured.
> Maybe, she is granting you a stab at eternity.
> The gothic vault of your bowels muttered dankly that this should be possible.
> I have no doubt the walls of that chamber will outlive the outline of my years.
> Indeed, you have the privilege of a preservation order.
> I wonder how that feels.
> However, it does not cover your un-architectured harmony –
> Your stone meeting leaf, your beam meeting branch and your light meeting shadow.
> Thank you for greeting me informally in your green pyjamas.
>
> You prompted the return of my ten-year-old eyes,
> And they skipped across your hidden contours – your playground just out of reach –
> Marvelling at how the fencing and scaffolding
> Had been absorbed into your present aesthetic.
> You have relaxed towards a more organic manifestation.
> The neatness of your octagonal inception has given way to a more interesting state –
> A wondrous new integrity, a lounging rather than a standing.
> A folly has no mission
> But is designed to make a statement – a kind of ta-dah, this is me
> But now there is more of a yawn and a laid back I am here in this wooded place.
> I am glad I can only glimpse you through the trees, glad that I am fenced out
> And that the tendrils of my imagination alone can enter.

This sense of peace and comfort can also be seen in one of the reflections:

> I sat for some time in the chapel which is beautiful and calm offering a sense of peace. The chapel seemed to glorify nature with lots of animal wooden carving in the architrave and flowers in the ceramic tiles. The

little wooden seats were comfortable and warm and when the sun shone it lit up the room.

The workshops were described within the context of a welcoming and friendly group and a warm congenial place:

> "On returning to the boardroom, images and ideas of *ma* in our heads, we were going to make a collagraph which is a type of printing plate made up of collaged elements, but it doesn't withstand many prints as it breaks down over time. In fact, the process felt like a metaphor for a life!"
>
> "The idea of *ma* stayed with us, and throughout the weeks of the project became a frame of reference for the group, where we spoke about the need to have a little *ma* time, and a recognition that this space in which we gathered and the time that we had together offered us just this thing."
>
> "Making simple collagraphs, adding foraged bits of nature from the walk, completely absorbed us for the whole morning. We forgot what time it was and I didn't want to break it up by having to eat lunch. Sometimes – hardly speaking to one another, then other times (around cups of tea!) we chatted and laughed. It was a lovely feeling to be part of a group again. Working side by side in good company, seeing the individuality of expression was fascinating. No stress or pressure to talk or compare."

At the end of the workshops a tree trail was developed with trees identified and small pieces of writing about them on wooden plaques. There was also an exhibition in the chapel.

> "He talked about how walking through the trees, winding one's way along the trail, can change one's sense of being, becoming a little more aware and perhaps calmer."
>
> "At the end of the workshops we went for a walk along the tree trail, my ankle no longer causing me a problem. I saw the trees differently, they were awesome, the Wellingtonias strong and majestic, the yews eerie and foreboding, the monkey puzzle tree tall and funny, the magnolia like a pretty ballerina making a curtsey."

Tryst

Lithe limbs of light
  entwine
    with lithe limbs of bough.
The above romances
  the below

in a sylvan cathedral
of chiaroscuro.

Waking breath of sky
commingles
with dreaming breath of wood –
so many kisses
in the mist –
the language of dawn
is silently understood.

Actions

So how do we take our understanding forward to support and develop mental wellbeing in ourselves and others? Four methods have been considered in this book related to the concepts in the chapters where they were presented:

- Resilience
- Art therapy
- Compassion-focused therapy
- Focusing

Resilience

Resilience, as explored in Chapter 3, is politically a very popular approach advocated by government, mental health services and education. Contemporary culture, with the hegemony of 'people are responsible for themselves and have the power to maintain and manage their personal wellbeing', would promote resilience training. However in the UK with its mixed economy this is rather blurred at times due to social care and the National Health Service.

Resilience can be conceived as:

- Personality traits: optimistic, curious, conceptualisation of problems
- Social network: good support networks such as family members, friends
- Process: learnt strategies
- Motivational force: behavioural drive

Resilience, whether regarded as personality traits, a process or a bio-psychosocial matrix, has been found to actively enhance positive psychological wellbeing (Davydov *et al.* 2010). There is some evidence to suggest resilience can be developed through cognitive behavioural therapy (CBT) training workshops regardless of its conception. CBT is based on the assumption that all behaviours are learnt, therefore if a person demonstrates less than 'normal' levels of resilience or maladaptive behaviours, therapeutic teaching or conditioning should improve functioning. Using CBT, a therapist assumes that dysfunctional underlying assumptions are the foundation for mental distress in times of adversity.

Therefore, CBT workshops could teach:

- Cognitive appraisal skills – lead the person to reassess the situation
- Stress management techniques – defusing catastrophic thinking, dealing with counterproductive beliefs, cognitive problem solving
- Developing social support networks
- Enhanced coping strategies

(Stewart and Terry 2014)

If this approach is to be used to help people gain mental wellbeing there are some questions a practitioner needs to ask:

1 Does it address all elements of mental wellbeing?
2 Does it address this person's mental wellbeing needs?
3 What are the disadvantages of undertaking this therapy?
4 In addition, any service will need to ask if the therapy is economically viable.

This therapeutic approach is individualistic; it assumes the person is not functioning at an optimal level and seeks to redress this. Contemporary society is, though, so concerned with the extent of mental distress in young people that teaching sessions on resilience and wellbeing are being initiated for children and young people as part of compulsory education. These sessions are economic and can facilitate young people having additional life skills, but they may have negative implications for self-esteem and the assumed link between thoughts and mood may not be a strong as expected. There may be a mismatch between cognition and mood; the person learns new strategies, but they continue to have a low mood.

People accessing these therapeutic techniques to develop resilience may use them in a developmental way; they are not usually unwell before starting. The aim of this approach is to reduce the risk of ill health. Given this aim it may not have the negative consequence of the person feeling guilty for their lack of skills that other individualistic therapies are prone to (see Table 3.1).

Compassion-focused therapy

Compassion-focused therapy (Gilbert 2009) was briefly described in Chapter 3. It is an integrated approach that is underpinned by several theoretical approaches: evolutionary, social, developmental and Buddhist psychology and neuroscience. Gilbert highlighted that people who were unable to feel self-compassion experience low levels of mental wellbeing. Compassion-focused therapy (CFT) seeks to rebalance the affective systems called affiliative focused, threat focused and incentive focused to enhance self-soothing in a frightening world.

When people feel unsafe and threatened, basic evolutionary responses in their brain occur, focusing on self-protection (threat focused) and turning off the self-soothing (affiliative focused) responses. This can cause the person to be cruel to themselves or others. CFT acknowledges that the person may realise they need to behave compassionately towards themselves or others but biologically (due to their neurological affective systems) or socially (social pressure) they are unable to do this.

CFT involves CBT type training, as outlined above, but the teaching is offered in an environment of warmth, kindness and support, as indicated by Rogers in his client-centred therapy. The focus of CFT is to teach the person to generate an emotion towards themselves of self-warmth or self-kindness, self-compassion. CFT therefore offers education within a warm and kind environment where compassion can also be learnt through role modelling. Self-compassion leads to mental wellbeing. Again, a practitioner will need to ask themselves some questions about the therapy before undertaking or recommending it.

1 Does it address all elements of mental wellbeing?
2 Does it address this person's mental wellbeing needs?
3 What are the disadvantages of undertaking this therapy?
4 In addition, any service will need to ask if the therapy is economically viable.

This therapeutic approach is again individualistic but there is a prominence of a compassionate therapeutic relationship between practitioner and troubled person. It offers the skill development as with CBT and Social Learning Theory (role modelling – see Chapter 2) alongside a therapeutic environment. Whilst using CFT is an attempt to address all the dimensions of wellbeing it is limited by its focus on change and therefore more concerned with the future (one part of temporality) than past or present.

Art therapy

Art therapy was briefly explored in Chapter 5; it involves creative activity and art-making processes targeting cognitive, motor, emotional and interpersonal skills. It serves as a non-verbal expressive medium, which offers insights into the 'inner world' through a three-way process between the person, the therapist and art resources (BAAT 2019).

Huss (2017) identified that art therapy can be conceptualised through all psychological and cultural perspectives. Each theoretical model tends to focus on the process and context of art activities, or art as an analytical tool.

Her multi-layered model has been developed to integrate the different theoretical conceptualisations, allowing each prism to add to the engagement, intervention and understanding of the areas of concern for the person (Huss 2017).

1 Does it address all elements of mental wellbeing?
2 Does it address this person's mental wellbeing needs?
3 What are the disadvantages of undertaking this therapy?
4 In addition, any service will need to ask if the therapy is economically viable.

Art can be used as a meaningful activity and provide a mechanism for wellbeing without any therapeutic intention. It can be a hobby that gives pleasure and production which are dimensions of wellbeing. Art therapy was developed to help those who are struggling to develop or maintain their sense of wellbeing and has been used within mental health services for many decades. It can be used as an assessment tool or as a therapeutic intervention for groups or individuals. How it is used will depend on the therapeutic style or perspective of the practitioner. This will also influence the advantages and disadvantages of the therapy.

Art therapy per se has a limited evidence base despite being generally acknowledged as helpful for people who are mentally unwell. It can be accessed as part of CBT, which has a significant but mixed evidence base as a distractor, for relaxation or reward. It can be used within dynamic psychotherapy as a means to explore the subconscious mind in a similar manner as free association or dream analysis. It can also be used in a humanistic way, which is one method for describing how the Stiwdio Arts Group functions with a therapeutic environment where space is given for self-recognition and non-judgemental positive regard is shared.

Focusing

From his collaboration with Carl Rogers Gendlin developed a process called 'focusing', a method for paying attention to one's own body. This process facilitated Gendlin's exploration of the extent to which people used their felt sense in their daily lives. Felt sense is a living interaction with the world. The more people are in tune with their felt sense, their experience of being alive in the world, the greater their opportunity for wellbeing. Felt sense can be developed through focusing. Focusing leads to greater awareness described as '*presence*' which can facilitate the development of a compassionate, accepting relationship. Bio-Spiritual Focusing, developed by Roman Catholic priests Peter Campbell and Edwin McMahon, similarly describes a caring, feeling presence and its ability to welcome whatever a person is with kindness and acceptance.

There have been a number of methods described as focusing but Gendlin proposed a process of:

1 Clear a space
2 Locate felt sense
3 Find a handle – descriptive words or images
4 Resonate word or image with felt sense
5 Receive the shift that occurs due to this realisation

But Foxcroft's (2005) process may offer greater clarity described as listening to one's self with compassion and offers the following phases:

1 Deciding – turning to the source
2 Resonating – the place has a unique feel, quality, mood or tone
3 Sensing-and-welcoming – returning to the body to look for a fit with a word, image, sound or gesture

This approach can clearly be seen to have developed from the foundations of Rogers' client-centred therapy where he provides the therapeutic space for the person to explore themselves and find their own meanings, self-acceptance, knowledge of their unique potential and their need to work towards this. What Gendlin and Foxcroft are doing is giving the person guidance on how to make (felt) sense of their world so that they can then move towards self-acceptance or in Todres' words a soulful space and dwelling mobility.

1 Does it address all elements of mental wellbeing?
2 Does it address this person's mental wellbeing needs?
3 What are the disadvantages of undertaking this therapy?
4 In addition, any service will need to ask if the therapy is economically viable.

Focusing as a therapeutic approach is a problem for services as, like CCT, it is open ended; the client stops attending when they feel they no longer need the therapist. Despite this it could be provided as teaching with the person practising alone; there does not seem to be a need for others to be involved once the person understands what needs to be done, as with CBT.

Stiwdio Arts Group

The Stiwdio Arts Group's achievements can be understood as an integration of different psychological perspectives under an umbrella of psychological phenomenology, accepting the current philosophical thinking relating to self-acknowledgement and self-acceptance recognising that personal experiences are contextual. This has been achieved through creative engagement and

Table 8.3 Types of wellbeing using the philosophy of 'dwelling-mobility' adapted from Galvin and Todres (2011) with examples from Stiwdio Arts Group

	Mobility	*Dwelling*	*Dwelling-mobility*
Spatiality	**Adventurous horizons** Example: *Learning new areas and art, history and meeting people*	**At homeness** Example: *I sat at the long table with a coffee. I felt as if I could be comfortable there forever*	**Abiding expanse** Example: *As a group we had gone on a journey of sorts, and we had been creating and working together towards our portrait of this family*
Temporality	**Future orientation** Example: *Reaching that bit further every time and exploring the materials that we use anew*	**Present-centredness** Example: *Where we spoke about the need to have a little ma time, and a recognition that this space in which we gathered and the time that we had together offered us just this thing*	**Renewal** Example: *A wondrous new integrity, a lounging rather than a standing*
Inter-subjectivity	**Mysterious interpersonal attraction** Example: *Louise's elderly mother was with us, she immediately made me feel strong, caring and capable*	**Kinship and belonging** Example: *I felt I also belonged to the group. I wasn't experiencing this on my own.* *We were surprised with how detailed but similar our views were*	**Mutual complementarity** Example: *Recognition that this space in which we gathered and the time that we had together offered us just this thing;* *The work we produce is a gift to be treasured, because of the journey we have had together*
Mood	**Excitement or desire** Example: *Sometimes – hardly speaking to one another, then other times, (around cups of tea!) we chatted and laughed*	**Peacefulness** Example: *This is a wonderful place of hope and healing, of love and laughter*	**Mirror-like multi-dimensional fullness** Example: *Working side by side in good company, seeing the individuality of expression was fascinating. No stress or pressure to talk or compare*

continued

Table 8.3 continued

	Mobility	*Dwelling*	*Dwelling-mobility*
Identity	**I can** Example: *I feel myself grow, as an artist, as a person.*	**I am** Example: Draw things, instead of having to talk about things, lose yourself in the doing. Being reminded that I'm pretty much normal, feeling better for it	**Layered continuity** Example: *It was about being with people who accepted me for who I am but also the alone times*
Embodiment	**Vitality** Example: *But it was more than that, it was a more visceral experience*	**Comfort** Example: *Lifts my spirits and gives my body a bit of peace to get on with getting better;* *Gives time and space enough to be still enough to reorientate my being*	**Grounded vibrancy** Example: *Once it had all come to an end, the sense of achievement and positivity did enhance the way I felt. It felt great that I had taken time out for myself, guilt-free to release those feelings of being stuck*

facilitation of dwelling mobility. The leaders developed this therapeutic environment where human flourishing was propagated.

Participation in this group was voluntary but people still entered the process with some anxiety; despite this, all engaged and can be considered to have experienced a felt sense of moments of soulful space. This was achieved through the experience of '*presence*'. This was initially provided by Louise and later between others in the interpersonal space. Presence facilitated the development of compassionate, accepting relationships leading to experiences of shared joy mediated by the body, truth, beauty and the divine. This is perhaps most aptly expressed by one participant who wrote:

> The process was surprising with elements of chance ever-present. Engaging, intriguing, magical and relaxing!

Summary

Mental wellbeing is subjective which makes it difficult to precisely define and measure. Many attempts have been made to do so but each falls short of providing a neat impression of the rich tapestry that facilitates this individual experience. This chapter has offered four categories of keys to mental wellbeing and ten dimensions, all of which are acknowledged as inadequate. Despite their inadequacy they were useful in identifying that the evaluations and reflections generated from the Stiwdio Art projects did demonstrate achievement of mental wellbeing for the participants given contemporary understanding of it.

The chapter's pathway led the reader to consider the concept of flourishing, the current understanding of it and if it could be recognised in the writings of the participants. This was indeed the case leading to the proposal that mental wellbeing is achieved *through lived experiences of shared joy mediated by the body, truth, beauty and/or the divine; this makes suffering in life experiences meaningful and life worthwhile.*

Throughout the chapter it is acknowledged that there is more to experiences than can be objectively stated and measured, and this was also true for the relationship between self and mental wellbeing with personality being defined as *the interaction between an individual's 'felt sense' which provides meaning through embodied relational knowing and the world in which the person lives in time and space.*

It is proposed here that a recognition of an embodied subjective self within a psychological phenomenological perspective offers greater opportunity for flourishing and mental wellbeing. Self-recognition and acceptance of one's self including personal vulnerability may be the first step towards self-compassion and mental wellbeing.

Mental wellbeing occurs through the ability to enter a moment in time and space, a '*soulful space*' where the person can accept themselves, in their entirety, including their vulnerability, to gain a deep sense of who they are and who they are becoming. It is through acceptance of self and others within a state of temporal and spatial *dwelling mobility* that people need to understand themselves and their personal present, history and future possibilities but also how this interweaves with their sense of others and others' history.

Conclusion

Dwelling mobility, soulful space and felt sense have much to offer understanding of mental wellbeing as concepts. This approach opens the lifeworld to the full possibilities of human potential.

Therapeutic approaches such as resilience training, compassion-focused therapy, art therapy and focusing can all add to understanding and the development of mental wellbeing, but 'presence' would appear to be key: to be truly accepting and accepted, to be loved and to love and in the moment experiencing a sense of joy and peace, acknowledging things will change, knowing it was achieved in the past, in the now and the future is full of possibilities.

References

Barker, S. 2018. "Embodied Recovery Environment" in Norman, I. and Ryrie, I. (Eds.) *The Art and Science of Mental Health Nursing*. London: OUP, Chapter 10.

Barker, S., Williams, S. 2018. "Compassionate Communication in Mental Health Care". *In*: Wright, K.M. and McKeown, M. (Eds.) *Essentials of Mental Health Nursing*. London: Sage, Chapter 20.

Burns, R.A., Machin, M.A. 2013. "Psychological Wellbeing and the Diathesis Stress Hypothesis Model: The Role of Psychological Functioning and Quality of Relations in Promoting Subjective Well-being in a Life Events Study", *Personality and Individual Differences*, 54, 3, 321–326.

Davydov, D.M., Stewart, R., Ritchie, K., Chaudieu, I. 2010. "Resilience and Mental Health", *Clinical Psychology Review*, 30, 479–495.

Department of Health (DoH). 2007. Commissioning Framework for Health and Wellbeing, p. 99. www.visionuk.org.uk/download/archive_1/pdf/PDF%20health%20and%20well(1).pdf

Foxcroft, R. 2005. Touching the Source. www.focusing.org.uk/touching-the-source.

Friedman, J. 1992. "The Past in the Future: History and the Politics of Identity", *American Anthropologist*, 94, 4, new series, 837–859. Retrieved from: www.jstor.org/stable/680224.

Fuchs, T. 2013. "Temporality and Psychopathology", *Phenomenology and the Cognitive Sciences*, 12, 75–104. DOI: 10.1007/s11097-010-9189-4.

Galvin, K.T., Todres, L. 2011. "Kinds of Well-being: A Conceptual Framework that Provides Direction for Caring", *International Journal of Qualitative Studies on Health and Well-being*, 6, 4. DOI: 10.3402/qhw.v6i4.10362.

Gendlin, E.T. 1987. "A Philosophical Critique of the Concept of Narcissism: The Significance of the Awareness Movement". *In*: Levin, D.M. (Ed.) *Pathologies of the Modern Self: Postmodern Studies on Narcissism, Schizophrenia and Depression.* New York: New York University Press, pp. 257–304.

Gilbert, P. (2009) "Introducing Compassion-focused Therapy", *Advances in Psychiatric Treatment*, 15, 199–208.

Huss, E. 2017. *A Theory-based Approach to Art Therapy. Implications for Teaching, Research and Practice.* London: Routledge.

Mathews, G., Izquierdo, C. (Eds.) 2009. *Pursuits of Happiness: Well-being in Anthropological Perspective.* New York: Berghahn.

Nicholls, D., Kidd, K., Threader, J., Hungerford, C. 2015. "The Value of Purpose Built Mental Health Facilities: Use of the Ward Atmosphere Scale to Gauge the Link between Milieu and Physical Environment", *International Journal of Mental Health Nursing*, 24, 286–294.

Nicholson, P. 2018. "Family Trees, Selfies and Our Search for Identity", *The Psychologist*, November 2018. Leicester: British Psychological Society.

Ryan, R.M., Deci, E.L. 2001. "On Happiness and Human Potentials: A Review of Research on Hedonic and Eudaimonic Well-being", *Annual Review of Psychology,* 52, 141–166. DOI: 10.1146/annurev.psych.52.1.141.

Stewart, W., Terry, L. 2014. "Reducing Burnout in Nurses and Care Workers in Secure Settings", *Nursing Standard,* 28, 34, 37–45.

Tay, L., Pawelski, J.O., Keith, M.G. 2018. "The Role of the Arts and Humanities in Human Flourishing: A Conceptual Model", *The Journal of Positive Psychology*, 13, 3, 215–225. DOI: 10.1080/17439760.2017.1279207.

Thomas, J. 2009. Working Paper: Current Measures and the Challenges of Measuring Children's Wellbeing. Newport: Office for National Statistics.

Todres, L. 2004. "The Wound that Connects: A Consideration of 'Narcissism' and the Creation of Soulful Space", *Indo-Pacific Journal of Phenomenology*, 4, 1, July.

Todres, L. 2007. *Embodied Enquiry: Phenomenological Touchstones for Research, Psychotherapy and Spirituality.* Basingstoke: Palgrave Macmillan.

Todres, L., Galvin, K. 2010. "'Dwelling-mobility': An Existential Theory of Well-being", *International Journal of Qualitative Studies on Health and Well-being*, 5, 3. DOI: 10.3402/qhw.v5i3.5444.

Wright, P.R., Robin Pascoe, R. 2015. "Eudaimonia and Creativity: The Art of Human Flourishing", *Cambridge Journal of Education*, 45, 3, 295–306. DOI: 10.1080/0305764X.2013.855172.

Index

Page numbers in **bold** denote tables, those in *italics* denote figures.

For Product Safety Concerns and Information please contact our EU representative GPSR@taylorandfrancis.com Taylor & Francis Verlag GmbH, Kaufingerstraße 24, 80331 München, Germany